GW00494428

Ordinary Wisdom

Reflections on an experiment in citizenship and health

Stella Davies, Susan Elizabeth, Bec Hanley,
Bill New and Bob Sang

Published by
King's Fund Publishing
11–13 Cavendish Square
London W1M 0AN

© King's Fund 1998

First published 1998

All rights reserved. No part of this publication may be reproduced, stored in a retrieval system or transmitted, in any form or by any means, electronic or mechanical, photocopying, recording and/or otherwise without the prior written permission of the publishers. This book may not be lent, resold, hired out or otherwise disposed of by way of trade in any form, binding or cover other than that in which it is published, without the prior consent of the publishers.

ISBN 1 85717 186 1

A CIP catalogue record for this book is available from the British Library

Available from:

King's Fund Bookshop
11–13 Cavendish Square
London W1M 0AN

Tel: 0171 307 2591

Printed and bound in Great Britain

Cover illustration: Mark Spain

Contents

Acknowledgements

We thank Anna Coote and Jo Lenaghan of the Institute of Public Policy Research for their willingness to share learning from their work in a consistently generous and supportive fashion. Their enthusiastic collaboration was vital to the success of our pilot juries.

Thanks are also due to Professor Albert Weale of Essex University, who first drew citizens' juries to the attention of the King's Fund Grants Committee and who, with his colleague Professor James Gobert, supported and constructively challenged the project team in equal measure throughout the course of the programme.

Our partners in the three health authorities – Sunderland, East Sussex and Buckinghamshire – shared the risk and the ultimate benefits of this important work.

Above all, this book is dedicated to the 45 'ordinary' citizens who found themselves part of an extraordinary experiment. Together they rose to the challenge with seriousness, commitment and great good humour. Our thanks to them.

Introduction

At the beginning of 1996 the Grants Committee at the King's Fund decided to invest £240,000 in a proactive grants programme that would evaluate the potential of citizens' juries as a means of public consultation within health authorities. The decision was in part a response to the innovative work that the Institute of Public Policy Research (IPPR) had recently begun on citizens' juries in the UK, but also was a natural evolution of the King's Fund's long-standing interest in user participation in the health field. Here was an opportunity to investigate the role of the citizen in health care policy and planning and how this might differ from the involvement of service users.

The grants programme was structured in two parts. A fieldwork programme, comprising three pilot citizens' juries in health authorities around the country (chosen from an original short list of six) was supplemented by an external independent evaluation of those three pilots and three other juries conducted by IPPR with health authorities during the summer of 1996. The juries sponsored by the King's Fund took place between January and March 1997 and were thus able to build on and incorporate learning from the earlier IPPR work. During 1996 the Local Government Management Board (LGMB) also ran a series of citizens' juries with local authorities around the country and we were able to share some informal learning.

The three sites chosen for the King's Fund juries, and their questions, were:

1. Sunderland Health Authority. '*A number of services are currently available from GPs. Would local people accept some of those services from any of the following: nurse practitioner; pharmacist; another (salaried) doctor?*'
2. East Sussex, Brighton & Hove Health Authority. '*Where should women with gynaecological cancer who live in East Sussex, Brighton & Hove be offered treatment?*'
3. Buckinghamshire Health Authority. '*Should Buckinghamshire Health Authority fund treatment from osteopaths and chiropractors for people with back pain?*'

The jury reports are presented in the Appendices, providing a helpful pen portrait of the content and process of the individual juries.

The project team drawn together at the King's Fund included both Fund personnel (Susan Elizabeth, Bill New, Bob Sang) and external staff bought in for their specific expertise (Bec Hanley, Stella Davies). Throughout the development and implementation of the citizens' juries, we worked within a framework of interlocking principles. We sought to build a model of citizens' juries that would:

- Support the legitimacy of the jury process among stakeholders and the wider public.
- Maximise the independence and integrity of the jury process.
- Respect diversity and difference of opinions among the jurors (avoiding the 'tyranny of the majority').
- Allow for the resolution of controversial issues.

Our interest in running the juries was to clarify the following key points:

- To assess the extent to which a citizens' jury approach is effective in promoting local democracy by enabling local people to:
    - (a) contribute to debates about the health services in their locality,
    - (b) have a positive influence on health policy in their locality.
- To assess the benefits and drawbacks of the citizens' jury approach from the perspective of health authorities, jurors and local interest groups.
- To contribute to a wider debate on issues of citizen participation by placing citizens' juries in the context of other systems and methods for public participation in health settings.

These points formed the basis of a brief to Shirley McIver at the Health Services Management Centre in Birmingham, who carried out an independent evaluation of the King's Fund and IPPR health-related citizens' juries. Her report, *Healthy Debate?*, answers these questions from the perspective of an independent and disinterested observer. This book, by contrast, is designed as a series of personal reflections from all those who took part in this important experiment in citizenship and health.

In the first chapter Bill New, researcher at the King's Fund, offers a historical perspective on the contribution that citizens' juries may make to democratic practice. He discusses four potential benefits to society and the individual citizen, and attempts to place the King's Fund programme within this framework. A clear understanding of the objectives of citizens' juries, he concludes, is essential if they are to survive the accusations that they are merely an elaborate and expensive charade.

In Chapter 2 the project managers at each of the three jury sites discuss their experience of managing a citizens' jury project within their health authority. They discuss their own reasons for wanting to run a citizens' jury and consider the complex network of relationships that each had to sustain in order to provide a successful environment in which the jury could work. They consider the importance of the role of an independent sponsor for the jury and conclude that there is a need to establish some system of accreditation for citizens' juries.

In Chapter 3 Bob Sang, of the King's Fund, and Stella Davies, an independent consultant, set out the model of facilitation that informed their work with all three juries. They set out their awareness that the jury process operated simultaneously at four levels and argue that it was essentially a model of adult learning whereby individual jurors engaged with witnesses in a mature and increasingly informed dialogue. They view this model of the jury process as *counter-cultural*, particularly in the NHS, but point out that it is an appropriate model for health policy decisions, which are full of ambiguity and uncertainty and where the evidence base is of highly variable reliability. They, too, look at the relationship between the independent sponsoring organisation and the participating health authorities and describe in detail the separate roles performed by the jury facilitators, that of 'the chair' and that of 'the juror's friend' enabling both task and process issues to be dealt with.

Chapter 4 charts the views of 16 jurors from the three different citizens' juries at a review meeting six months after the juries had taken place. Using the 'jury journey' as a metaphor, they reflect on the experience of being selected to take part in this experiment and its impact on their views on health policy decision-making, on citizenship and on their own personal development.

Finally, in Chapter 5 Bob Sang seeks to place citizens' juries in the wider context of public involvement methods used in the health sector.

So what has the King's Fund learned from this work about the potential of citizens' juries in the health sector? In our reflections on the work, we have returned again and again to three key areas of difficulty. First, there is the question of how the decisions of the group of sixteen people, however carefully selected, can have legitimacy and in what ways the citizen jury process can be constructed so as to maximise the potential for legitimacy. Second, there are considerable concerns about the cost-effectiveness of citizens' juries. Our experience shows them to be an expensive model of participation, although some health authority participants clearly thought that the quality of the outcome justified the cost. Third, there are significant questions surrounding the implementation of jury recommendations. At the time of writing it is too early to trace the progress of jury decisions through the health authority planning and decision-making processes. However, it is also clear that the task of monitoring implementation and decisions did not fall naturally to any existing group or agency. In some cases, the jurors themselves have kept up pressure on the health authority, but others see this as an undesirable development that absorbs the juror (originally valued as a truly independent voice) into the structures and processes of health care decision-making on a continuing basis.

In the light of our learning from the citizens' juries programme, we suggest the following as indicating when it would be appropriate for a health authority to hold a citizens' jury:

- there is lack of consensus in the host organisation about the answer to a particular contentious question;
- existing mechanisms to reach consensus have proved unsatisfactory;
- the organisation genuinely wants to answer the question;
- the organisation is open to a range of answers to the question;
- the organisation acknowledges that the public has a genuine and legitimate interest in the question;
- the question that needs to be addressed is at a strategic level and has significant operational implications;
- the organisation supports innovation and significant investment in local provision.

Above all, throughout this programme of experimentation with citizens' juries we have affirmed that citizens are able, and ready, to engage as peers with professionals on questions of health care policy. Even if citizens' juries do not become widely used, the distinctive principles they embody might be adapted to influence the ways in which the public participates in health matters in the future. Within a consultation framework that provides, in Anna Coote's words, *'information, time, scrutiny, deliberation, independence and authority'*[1] health authorities can learn to trust, and work with, the ordinary wisdom of local citizens.

Susan Elizabeth, Director of Grants, King's Fund

---

1   Coote A, Lenaghan J. *Citizens' juries: theory into practice.* London: Institute for Public Policy Research, 1977.

Chapter 1

Citizens' juries: empowerment, self-development, informed view or arbitration?

Bill New

The state of Britain's democracy is under scrutiny, and our health care system is no exception. The media are obsessed with the NHS: stories of declining standards, regional variations and individuals refused treatment fuel public concern. There is a growing sense of insecurity and public confidence seems to be ebbing. Trust in politicians may never have been lower.[1]

Many now argue that a contributory factor to this 'dysfunctional democracy' is the tenuous relationship between the public and policy-makers.[2] Most decisions in the NHS are taken, in the context of government regulation, at local level by individual health authorities, GP fundholders and trusts. These bodies are formally accountable – directly or indirectly – to the Secretary of State for Health, who in turn answers to Parliament. Every few years the people can vote for a new government, but this is the only formal power that citizens have to influence decisions about health. Two further mechanisms (non-executive directors of health authorities and trusts, and community health councils) provide limited opportunities for indirect public participation. Finally, there is the possibility of protest and influence: lobbying, demonstrating and pressure group activity.

In recent years, however, innovation in participatory democratic practice has blossomed.[3] Citizens, and more commonly users of health services, are increasingly being invited to take part in panels, conferences, service development meetings and surveys. Citizens' juries form one element in this constellation and – perhaps because of their arresting name – have caught the imagination of policy commentators and public sector managers. Much of the written analysis has been positive, viewing the juries as an exciting new method of addressing some of the deficiencies of the UK's democratic system.[4]

How juries work, what they do and the details of the King's Fund's pilot series are covered elsewhere in this volume. In this chapter the focus is on what citizens' juries might seek to achieve. It transpires that there a number of potential objectives, not all of which are compatible but all relating in some way to how we understand democracy. It is a troublesome concept: we all support democracy but it is a vague and elusive term, capable of being attached to quite distinct and incompatible activities.

In the first section, the meanings of some important terms are briefly reviewed, including the elusive nature of 'democracy' itself. In the second section some competing concepts of democratic participation are analysed, from the ancient Greeks to more recent innovations. Finally, the relationship between these concepts and the practice of running citizens' juries is discussed.

Some perspectives on democracy and the 'lay citizen'

Democracy is a notoriously difficult concept to pin down. An essential element is the notion that the general public have a degree of ultimate sanction over political decisions, rather than decision-making processes ending with a single autocratic individual or with a small elite group. But the 'people' are involved only intermittently in a formal sense, and when they are it is usually only to vote for representatives. Who these representatives are, how the rules governing the processes by which they are elected are formed, and how those who exercise judicial power are chosen – all these elements of a political system have little formal and direct link to the public. Neither do citizens have formal sanction over the decisions of representatives between elections.

But formal power is only part of the story. Equally important is the ability of citizens to take part in open debate, to dissent and protest, to have access to information, and to challenge rulers to explain their actions.[5] So, participating in decision-making by means of mechanisms such as the citizens' jury might reasonably be considered 'democratic' even though it does not involve formal power.

More generally, democracy should not be mistaken for politics.[6] Democracy is certainly a style of politics, and it is one that is more or less indispensable in modern states, the style being some combination of the elements described above. But a political system may operate without the formal involvement of the people in order to preserve the community, particularly in dire circumstances such as war. Furthermore, democracy, improperly and partially conceived, can go beyond politics. If we adopt the principal element of a democracy – individual voting power – and ignore the refining characteristics, we can easily end up with forms of elective tyranny. If substantial, and regular, votes are taken on public issues, and the results are decided on the basis of simple majorities, we no longer have a system of discussion, debate and reflection – or at least this is not assured. Minority views can legitimately be ignored. Diverse, vibrant and dynamic societies may be unsustainable where democracy is taken to extremes.

Finally, we should reflect briefly on the nature of our 'lay citizen'. 'Lay' according to a dictionary definition means: *'pertaining to the people . . . non-professional'*. Where citizens are involved, therefore, the style of politics moves from one in which experts, specialists and professionals dominate – Plato's captain of the ship of state – to one in which those who have no special, vested or pecuniary interest are given influence. People are of course 'interested' in their community, in social justice, in freedom, and so on. But for most people these matters are not of primary importance. Most of a citizen's time is spent worrying about work, or in finding a loving partner and bringing up a family, or deciding how to spend his or her income. The actions of government influence these activities to a significant degree, but they rarely pertain directly and persistently. When they do, the citizen may become an activist, for example, or join a political party. But, typically, the conduct of politics is a part-time concern – a luxury for many people who have more immediate daily pressures and worries.

Many believe that this distancing from political activity has gone too far, resulting in a resentful and suspicious public who can no longer respect, trust or engage with political leaders. This is a serious worry. Nevertheless, any view of the future role of the citizen should acknowledge that it will remain distinct from that of the paid, professional rulers who have chosen to devote their lives to public service. In the citizens' jury experiment, this distinction is important. Although wishing to reinvigorate the individual citizen's trust in political processes, the objective was not to persuade them to change their career. The 'lay' nature of their involvement – their 'ordinariness' to paraphrase the title of this book – was considered a positive virtue and should be retained.

Concepts of democratic participation

The various historical concepts of democratic practice reveal a diverse set of potential benefits to society and the individual citizen, not all of which are mutually compatible. Four have been chosen to structure the analysis that follows: empowerment, self-development, 'informed view' and arbitration.

There may be others but these four offer a reasonable representation of the many different views on what makes democracy essential for the conduct of a mature society.

The first, and most obvious, objective of democratic participation is to give power to the people. This had perhaps its fullest realisation in ancient Athens, still a system to marvel at for many modern democrats. All 'citizens' of Athens were entitled – indeed expected – to take an active part in decisions concerning public order, taxation and foreign matters.[7] Athenian citizens gathered together more than 40 times a year to discuss these matters in the hope of reaching consensus or, where this proved impossible, to vote on the best way forward.

One reason why such an extraordinary system of direct democracy could operate successfully was the limited concept of a 'citizen'. Most Athenian residents were slaves – 80,000–100,000 in total – and outnumbered free citizens by a proportion of 3:2. Other groups were also unable to participate. Women had no political rights; 'immigrants', who might have settled two or three generations earlier, were excluded, as were young men under the age of 20. In short, the political class was a highly homogenous group, allowing for more agreement on political issues than one would have found in the population as a whole.

Not everyone was enamoured of Athenian democracy, however, and for reasons other than its exclusivity. Plato and Aristotle, no less, were both hostile, arguing that such mechanisms of conducting public life led to rash, impetuous decisions; encouraged support for those who were most articulate, wealthy and persuasive rather than competent; and led to instability and incoherence in law-making. For although the system encouraged face-to-face debate, and therefore in principle reflective and considered analysis, the sheer number of participants inevitably led to the formation of factions. Opinions were formed in a highly charged atmosphere, perhaps as a result of an emotive speech specifically designed to carry a particular vote.

Plato, in particular, saw good political rule as something that ought to be undertaken by people with competence and experience. Democracy, he argued, encourages political leaders to take the easy option to preserve their popularity, rather than recognise the unpleasant truth on which sound political judgement depends. Plato, of course, argued for philosopher kings to act as 'guardians' of the common good. This conclusion is now regularly cited with ridicule as hopelessly out of date and reactionary. The rhetorical question

– 'who guards the guardians?' – reflects a fundamental flaw in Plato's vision: checks are needed on power to prevent its corruption. But other elements of his critique are still relevant today, particularly those that relate to ill-considered decision-making, and have been influential in the development of citizens' juries.

Nevertheless, the goal of handing 'real' power to the people persists. Use of the referendum is one, apparently impeccable, way of directly involving the citizen. So direct, in fact, that there is little or no mediation between the citizen and the decision. For those who promote the benefits of the referendum and 'direct democracy', it constitutes the natural endpoint of the development of democracy from Athenian models, through the representative system, to a utopian future where, thanks to modern communication techniques, all citizens can continuously vote on matters of public interest. The role of political representatives could, in principle, be reduced to that of democratic managers and administrators who simply implement decisions made by the public.

The referendum is used regularly in some US states and in Switzerland, as well as occasionally in many other countries, usually on matters of constitutional importance. But it is also criticised strongly on a number of counts: the proposition may be crudely phrased, voters may lack relevant information, there is no requirement for reflective and rational consideration, powerful financial interests may dominate campaigns, minority rights may be compromised, and so on.[8]

The call for direct (voting) democracy tends to come from the political Right – partly because of its mistrust of state institutions, which are viewed as seeking to promote their own ends at the taxpayer's expense.[9] Shifting power directly to the taxpayer allows a more 'realistic' assessment of the trade-offs between higher public spending and lower taxes. In contrast, the political Left has typically been more concerned about the effect such mechanisms would have on the marginalised in society who have special needs but insufficient voting power to make their interests count in a crude political marketplace. The Left's vision of direct citizen empowerment has therefore been rather different.

Karl Marx never provided an adequate theory, or even description, of the institutional features that would characterise a communist future, but all the indications are that he favoured some kind of direct democracy. He took as his cue the experience of the 1871 Paris Commune, and was probably inspired at least in part by the experience of ancient Greece. The Commune system involved each region electing delegates by universal suffrage. These delegates would elect further delegates for larger territorial areas, and so on, creating a pyramid structure. All delegates (not representatives) would be bound by the instructions of their constituency, and subject to immediate recall and re-election at all times.

Marx saw the need for these kinds of structure eventually dying out as the class-based nature of society withered away. Such a revolution has not, of course, taken place. Nevertheless, Marx's views on democracy, as on much else, have enjoyed a persistent influence ever since. The guiding principle is to prevent the separation of the rulers from the ruled, and instead to take all decisions collectively; whenever there is a need for greater individual political responsibility, this should be as a directly elected *delegate* whose position is at all times revocable. Thus political power is retained as close to the people as possible.

The Greek city-state that provided inspiration for these variants was essentially a moment in history, brought about by a particular mix of circumstances for one small portion of Europe around the fifth century BC. As concepts of who constitutes the citizenry – defined as those who are thought to have a direct interest in public affairs – widened, the practical possibility of bringing all these people together in one place receded. By the nineteenth century, and notwithstanding the forthcoming contribution of Marx, the terms of understanding democratic participation had fundamentally changed: from direct involvement in decision-making to the determination of political will through the medium of elected representatives. Representative democracy was seen as the grand solution to the problem of large, complex nation states, and the mass of conflicting interests within them.[10]

Out of these developments emerged a second understanding of participation – self-development. Rather than simply a means of wielding power, participating in political life would allow the individual citizen to develop and 'grow' as a mature, rational person, capable of contributing to and sustaining democracy itself. John Stuart Mill in particular supported this view: representative government offered the only way in which large, complex nation states could involve large numbers of individual citizens. It was

> an important aspect of the free development of individuality: participation in political life (voting, involvement in local administration and jury service) was vital to create a direct interest in government and, consequently, a basis for an involved, informed and developing citizenry. Mill conceived of democratic politics as a prime mechanism of moral self-development.[11]

Mill likened periodic voting to the action of a juror: a judgement on the performance of the government, the result of a considered process of reflection and rational analysis. It is interesting that jury service was specifically cited as an example – active citizenship was perceived as a duty as much as a right, without which democratic 'muscle' could not develop.

For Mill democratic involvement was, in part, an end in itself: participation sustains societies by promoting mature citizens capable of rational deliberation. Support for these ideas has persisted, but in the late twentieth century it was the perceived insufficiency of the traditional means of participation (voting, jury service) that sparked renewed interest in methods that might involve the citizenry for longer than it takes to vote or sit through a criminal trial.

The third view of democratic participation seeks the informed view of the citizen, and involves developing more sophisticated and participative methods for communicating the wishes and needs of the citizen than can occur through intermittent electoral contests. For example, in the past the options open to a citizen were to *'write to [a] Member of Parliament, work in a group to raise a local problem, go on a protest march, or canvass for a political party'*.[12] More recently, 'shared' decision-making has refined these traditional methods of lobby and protest. Citizens may now be invited into the decision-making system, given the time to think issues through and the opportunity to debate them with one another and with elected officials. They are formally engaged and 'designed in' to the processes by which decisions are made. For some in the health care field, this type of participation is becoming so important that they *'advocate the introduction of statutory duties which will make it clear in what circumstances the public and individual patients can expect to be involved in health and health-care decision-making'*.[13]

Numerous institutional forms are being developed, and the pace of change is such that a particular range of examples will rapidly become obsolete. A recent review included health panels, issues forums, deliberative opinion polls, future search conferences, and 'round tables'.[14] Partnership and involvement with individual clinical decision-making also constitute an important element in new forms of participation.[15] Here the decision-maker (the allocator of health care resources) is the clinician, who decides what treatment, if any, to give the patient. 'Patient partnership' has the patient sharing this decision-making process with the clinician, shaping what he or she receives or wishes not to receive. In essence, the common theme of these developments is that shared decision-making provides both a more considered and legitimate view from the citizen, while ensuring that those views and opinions are integrated into the decision-making process. Citizens are reassured that their opinions are heard in the heart of political institutions, bolstering support for democracy itself.

For all these optimistic visions, such developments are not accompanied by any real clarity about the degree of authority handed over to the citizen when they are involved in decision-making. These innovations do not empower the individual citizen in the manner of Athenian democracy. The health authority, for example, remains the final arbiter of how health care resources should be allocated. From this perspective, the involvement of the citizen constitutes a way to hear a clear, informed 'voice', but no more. Where interests, wants and needs have been poorly understood in the past, these participatory mechanisms are aimed at understanding them more clearly. Organised channels are designed for the better articulation of the citizen's voice, but it remains a voice that is merely 'one among many'.[16] Others – the professionals', the managers' – may still have greater influence.

The final form of democratic participation involves arbitration. The courtroom jury is not a political decision-making institution at all, and yet is seen as one of the cornerstones of modern democracies. The principle that one's guilt or otherwise in questions of law should be decided by fellow citizens – not by experts, bureaucrats or political representatives – is considered a fundamental buttress against state power. Lay people sit in judgement of one another, and only they possess the power to convict or acquit. Such an idea can be seen as profoundly democratic, even if the class privileges associated with the judicial system as a whole rather taint this view.

Perhaps the most important feature for our analysis of citizens' juries is that no expertise is deemed necessary for the lay citizen to be able to pronounce on matters that take place within a highly professionalised and technical context. Citizens' juries have no formal authority – inevitable perhaps, given the early stage of their development – but the principle remains the same: the lack of professional or expert knowledge can have an important role in retaining integrity when resolving contentious matters. It remains to be seen whether the non-factual nature of a citizens' jury's 'judgement' – on value-based public policy rather than on the factual matter of innocence or guilt – will be a permanent brake on its more widespread use.

Which objective for the citizens' jury?

As we have seen, citizens have been involved in democratic processes in a number of different ways and with a number of different rationales. Athenian and Marxist views see the people as being given real *power*, both to set an agenda and to control decisions that are made; there are no representatives, only delegates at most. The closest that modern societies get to such an objective is the referendum, which can be binding in certain circumstances.

Representation forms of democracy, for their part, see political power 'handed over' to representatives who then act according to their proclaimed ideals and promises; they can be rejected only at intermittent elections. Engaging with this process has been considered important in the development of a mature and active citizen – with *self-development*. Involvement acts to cultivate democratic 'muscle' by encouraging rational reflection and debate.

Ordinary citizens, in representation systems, are invited to participate, no matter how closely, simply to articulate their interests and concerns – as one voice among other interests in society who may feel they have a stake in an issue. Formal power, or even priority, is not accorded to lay citizens. The objective is to seek an *informed view* from citizens, not to relinquish power to them.

Finally, in the case of the courtroom jury, the objective is to involve citizens as *arbiters*. They are given real power and authority and their influence is direct, although not to set the agenda or even to influence the rules within which they work. They are tightly constrained as to the terms of their influence. Authority is real, but limited – it is used for the service of the state in conducting a very specific activity within the judicial system.

All four of these objectives have influenced the practical experience of running juries, and have contributed to the tensions and confusions in the debate about how they might contribute to improving democracy.

Empowerment

There was persistent uncertainty during the pilot series of citizens' juries as to the degree to which jurors should be given control of the agenda, the power to select witnesses, and even the option of rejecting the question and considering instead one thought more suitable. The more radical of observers had pressed for the juries to be able to take as much control of the process as possible. At one extreme, this might have involved allowing jurors to choose the issue they wished to address. More commonly, there was disagreement about whether, and to what extent, the jury should be allowed to supply recommendations that were not solicited by the statutory agency involved, and, if so, what responsibility the agency had to respond to them.

At the very least, in all the King's Fund and IPPR juries, the jurors were given the opportunity to choose one or two witnesses for themselves, either to re-interrogate one they had already seen or to call for an entirely new witness of their choosing. More generally, and particularly in the King's Fund pilots, jurors were given a significant say over the 'ground rules' of process: whether they wished for certain sessions to be 'in camera', whether they felt comfortable with the number of observers, and so on. These issues are covered in detail in Chapter 3.

The most significant unresolved aspect in all the juries was the extent to which the jury could legitimately amend, or even ignore, the question posed. A careful reading of the jury reports in the Appendices reveals that on occasion the jury felt that the question was inappropriate, particularly in Buckinghamshire. In all the juries, recommendations were supplied that went beyond the remit of the original question.

Under current constitutional arrangements there is no prospect of responsibility for public affairs being formally handed over to a citizens' jury or any other small lay group. For this reason, real power will remain with statutory agencies. Nevertheless, juries are in a position to influence significantly the decisions these agencies take. They could also be offered real power to set their own agenda and run their own process. The issue for those who wish to encourage the latter is whether it will weaken the juries' impact on the statutory agency – who for their part may argue, regardless of their legal rights, that they have no moral or *de facto* obligation to respond to unsolicited recommendations.

Self-development

A conclusion that has enjoyed general consensus is that the jurors themselves found the experience to be immensely rewarding.[17] Although nervous and occasionally apprehensive at the outset of the process, and often not sure why this apparently weighty responsibility was being thrust upon them, the jurors almost unanimously agreed subsequently that they had personally benefited, and often claimed to have a renewed interest in public affairs. So, from Mill's point of view, the objective of democratic self-development would seem to have been wholeheartedly achieved.

There are, however, at least two difficulties. The first is that the number of people who are involved in a citizens' jury will be small. So, although it may well have a wider influence on the democratic health of society beyond the people directly involved – the wider community may feel reassured that a decision was taken 'democratically' – the effect on individual self-development in society as a whole will be minimal. Better than nothing, perhaps, and citizens' juries are in any case only one example in a range of participatory innovations in democratic practice. Nevertheless, it would be unwise to hope for seismic change in active citizenship on the basis of citizens' juries alone.

The second difficulty is that a concern with citizens' personal development could potentially compromise other objectives. Much emphasis in the King's Fund pilots was given to the well-being, comfort and security of the jurors. For example, closed sessions were instituted in which jurors and moderators worked alone on procedural matters, and much effort was devoted to controlling the activities of the press and other observers (again, see Chapters 3 and 4). Jurors were thus able to deliberate without distraction and to reach consensus successfully.

However, if a significant portion of the jury's time is spent in closed session, and therefore not open to scrutiny, its findings may lose authority as a consequence – the 'informed view' might seem tainted, for example. The commissioning agency might suspect that the conclusions of the jury have been biased in some way during these sessions. Furthermore, if jurors are made to feel too comfortable with one another, and therefore unwilling to challenge the opinions of their colleagues, productive and critical debate within the group might be inhibited. A balance has to be struck between ensuring both a safe, comfortable context for the jury to work in and the degree of openness and critical rationality on which democratic procedures depend.

Informed view

Perhaps not surprisingly, an 'informed view' tends to be the objective favoured by commissioning organisations. This concept of the purpose of citizens' juries is reflected in the comments of the health authorities themselves. The reasons for running a jury recorded in the formal evaluation of the pilot series included:

- obtaining an '*informed view . . . to compare with professionals*';
- a '*sensible view*';
- '*consultation*'; or
- as '*one stage in a wider consultation process*'.[18]

Health authorities retain responsibility for health care in their area and must account for it, so they retain the final decision-making power. At one level, therefore, it is not surprising that these authorities might see the citizens' jury as a very specialised form of public consultation, with the lay citizen simply 'one voice among many'.[19]

This concept was also reflected in the series run by the Local Government Management Board.[20] Here juries were provided with issues such as *'People take drugs – how can we reduce harm to the community and individuals?'* and, simply, *'Norwich in the computer age'*. The stated expectations of the commissioning authorities were to *'involve the community in local government test processes'* and *'obtain views on an issue and increase openness of policy making'*. Seeking an informed view is commonly associated with open-ended questions such as these, in which specific choices are not sought, and are amenable to other methods of involvement such as *'future search conferences'*.[21] In the jury context, this has been termed a 'deliberative' citizens' jury, in contrast to a 'decision-making' model that matches more closely the arbitration objective outlined below.[22]

People who view citizens' juries in this way are often sceptical about their potential. Ron Zimmern, Director of Public Health at Cambridge and Huntingdon Health Authority, argued that citizens' juries were really just

> *a glorified focus group. The only difference is that a greater amount of effort is spent educating the group beforehand, and it goes on for four days. What it did was to give me the views of those 16 people who took part . . . It was enlightening to gain information at first hand, but where I have a huge problem with citizens' juries is that those behind the idea want us to say that once citizens have given their view, then the health authority must explain itself if it does not accept the recommendation. There's no reason why an authority should come down in favour of what a citizens' jury says any more than what a group of doctors says.*[23]

Such a view places the role of participation in a jury as simply a sophisticated means of eliciting the 'voice' or opinion of the citizen, but which subsequently has no more weight than the view of any other group. It has even been suggested by Bob Worcester, the head of MORI, that the informed citizen view is invalid precisely *because* the vast mass of the people have not had an opportunity to deliberate on plentiful information and expert presentations.[24] The citizens' jury, rather than being an 'authentic' voice, is an erroneous voice.

The cost of citizens' juries, for these sceptics, severely limits their usefulness – far more comprehensive (if less sophisticated) surveys of public opinion could be achieved at less cost. This concept also implies that citizens' juries should not be constrained by accreditation mechanisms that seek to establish rules for their conduct: each agency, whether in the public or the private sector, should decide how they wish to hold and use a jury. Let a thousand flowers bloom because, in the end, their purpose is solely to *inform* the agency in question. It does not matter that they might be conducted in different ways according to different principles – perhaps less rigorous in avoiding bias, for example – because no wider interest is affected. (Such a view assumes that the agency would at least fund the jury, even if they did not run it. They would therefore simply account for their use of their own resources in undertaking a citizens' jury.)

Those who do seek accreditation and ground rules for running juries may not see the role of the jury as quite so limited. If juries are used as a means of legitimising certain forms of decision about how to use public funds, there would seem to be a case for ensuring that the procedure conforms to certain principles of due process: for example, that all interests with respect to an issue have an equal chance to present their case. In any event, the view that a jury is simply a 'glorified focus group' may conflict with the final of our four potential objectives.

Arbitration

The King's Fund pilots were designed in part to develop an aspect of the IPPR juries that showed promise, and was in sharp contrast to the LGMB series. The King's Fund only gave grants to those health authorities who wished to resolve an issue that involved choosing between clearly defined options, each of which – in theory at least – the authority was equally willing to adopt. This situation might arise because the standard process of policy decision-making, undertaken by the democratically nominated managerial and bureaucratic staff in the agency, had reached an impasse. 'Experts' can disagree, and elected representatives may not be able to decide which policy option to take, possibly because the arguments and interests concerned are finely balanced. In such circumstances, the argument runs, let a panel of disinterested lay people decide which option to adopt. The Appendices set out the questions and options offered to the juries in the King's Fund series.

As we have already noted, the jury's decision at no time had legal force and the authority could reject the decision and adopt its own course of action. But it was hoped that the juries' decisions would nevertheless carry weight and that the authority would at least explain fully why it could not, after all, go along with the recommendations. The jury, for their part, agreed to stick to the task assigned to them, uncomfortable as it might be and inevitably involving constraints on the recommendations they could make because of resource limits (limits set, in turn, by the commissioning authority). In this concept of the citizens' jury, the lay public *do* occupy a special place among other interest groups, based precisely on their lay position. They are disinterested, in a way similar to courtroom jurors, and can therefore bring impartiality and democratic legitimacy to the resolution of a contentious political problem.

This objective – of public policy arbitration – continually found itself in competition with all the other objectives outlined above. Health authorities were reluctant to accept publicly the juries' verdicts in advance, concerned perhaps that some recommendations would not be practical or affordable. In some cases there remained a suspicion that all the options were *not*, in fact, equally acceptable to the health authority (i.e. they had a favoured policy route that they fervently hoped the juries would validate!).

Part of the difficulty, on the other hand, may have been with the jury process itself. Leeway was given to jurors, in pursuit of other democratic objectives, to challenge the authority on matters outside the terms of the original question, to object to the nature of the question and to make recommendations well beyond that of the central issue. Such outcomes, though legitimate in themselves, leave the door open for authorities to claim that they were being pushed beyond their original 'contract' as well as potentially compromising their statutory obligations and resources.

Conclusion

The range of democratic objectives that juries might pursue has meant that those taking part – whether deliberating, commissioning, facilitating or merely observing – have brought with them a similarly wide range of aspirations and preconceptions as they engaged with the experiment. For example, the health authorities were acutely aware of their legal responsibility for the final decision taken on behalf of the whole community, and were therefore more likely to view the jury as providing merely an informed view. The King's Fund set up the process on the arbitration and self-development models, viewing the juries not simply as one voice among many but as a profoundly democratic body even if this was not formally binding on health authorities. During the process, those who actually facilitated the juries and who worked closely with them were deeply concerned that the jurors should be empowered wherever possible and that their self-development and 'learning' should be safeguarded.

There is no inevitable reason why these objectives should conflict. In particular, self-development could easily be seen as complementary to all the other objectives as long as it does not dominate the process. But it is less easy to accommodate other goals simultaneously and still retain clarity about the outcome being sought. This is not a criticism of the pilot series, or of the other series ran by the IPPR and LGMB, because these pilots were conducted precisely in order to uncover lessons for the future. Furthermore, this conclusion could well be applied to experimentation with citizen participation more generally.

Perhaps the principal lesson from this democratic experiment is that there must be clarity about the objective of any exercise in public participation, *before* it is embarked on. The alternative is that these exciting experiments may falter. Participatory democrats will continue to risk the accusation that these mechanisms are merely an elaborate and expensive charade – they will remain open to the stinging charge of 'window dressing'. The experience of those who took part in the King's Fund series is that citizens' juries can achieve more and deserve better.

References and notes

1   Curtice J, Jowell R. Trust in the political system. In: R Jowell *et al.* (eds). *British social attitudes*, 14th Report. Aldershot: Ashgate Publishing, 1997.

2   Cooper L, Coote A, Davies A, Jackson C. *Voices off: tackling the democratic deficit in health*. London: Institute for Public Policy Research, 1995.

3   Stewart J. *Further innovation in democratic practice*. Birmingham: Institute of Local Government Studies, 1996.

4   Coote A, Lenaghan J. *Citizens' juries: theory into practice*, London: Institute for Public Policy Research, 1997; Hall D, Stewart J. *Citizens' juries in local government: report for the LGMB on the pilot projects*. London: Local Government Management Board, 1996.

5   See Klein R, New B. *Two Cheers? Reflections on the health of NHS democracy*. London: King's Fund, 1998.

6   Crick B. *In defence of politics*. London: Penguin, 1982 (2nd edn).

7   Held D. *Models of democracy*. Cambridge: Polity Press, 1996.

8   Cronin TE. *Direct democracy: the politics of initiative, referendum and recall*. London: Harvard University Press, 1989.

9   Beedham D. Survey: full democracy. *The Economist*. 1996: 21 December.

10   Held D. Introduction: central perspectives on the modern state. In: Held D (ed.) *States and societies*. Oxford: Martin Robertson, 1983.

11 Ibid., p. 17.

12 Parry G, Moyser G, Day N. *Political participation and democracy in Britain,* Cambridge: Cambridge University Press, 1992, p. 4.

13 Barnes M. *The people's health service?* NHS Confederation research paper No 2. Birmingham: Health Services Management Centre, 1997.

14 Stewart J. *Further innovation in democratic practice.* Birmingham: Institute of Local Government Studies, University of Birmingham, 1996.

15 Farrell C, Gilbert H. *Health care partnerships: debates and strategies for increasing patient involvement in health care and health services.* London: King's Fund, 1996; Coulter A. Partnerships with patients: the pros and cons of shared clinical decision-making. *Journal of Health Services, Research and Policy* 1997; 2(2): 112–21.

16 Mort M, Harrison S, Dowsell T. Public health panels in the UK: influence at the margins? In: Kahn UA (ed). *Innovations in public participation.* London: UCL Press, 1998.

17 See Coote and Lenaghan, op cit., and Hall and Stewart, op cit.

18 These comments are taken from the formal evaluation of the King's Fund and IPPR series, and relate to juries run by both organisations: McIver S. *Healthy debate?* London: King's Fund, 1998.

19 See Mort *et al.*, op cit.

20 Hall and Stewart, op cit.

21 Sang R, Dubras M. *'Local everywhere': the use of whole system interventions.* King's Fund Report to the NHS Executive, January 1996.

22 Lenaghan J, New B, Mitchell E. Setting priorities: is there a role for citizens' juries? *British Medical Journal* 1996; 312: 1591–3.

23 Quoted in Snell. The rationing dilemma. *Health Management* 1997; March: 8–10.

24 Milne K. Politics. *New Statesman* 1996; 30 August: 8–9.

Chapter 2

Managing the organisational context for a citizens' jury

Maureen Dale, Bec Hanley, Gill Needham, Zoe Nicholson

The three health authorities awarded grants by the King's Fund appointed a project manager to take the lead in organising a citizens' jury. This chapter has been written by the project managers – Maureen Dale, Gill Needham and Zoe Nicholson – and by Bec Hanley, the King's Fund fieldworker. The project managers have different backgrounds and different roles in their health authority: Maureen is the Quality Manager for Sunderland Health Authority; Gill is the research and development specialist for Buckinghamshire Health Authority; Zoe is the Commissioning and Primary Care Development Manager for East Sussex, Brighton & Hove Health Authority. Bec works on a freelance basis on a variety of projects to support the involvement of citizens and users in decision-making about health. This chapter is based on our personal views, and does not necessarily reflect the views of the health authorities or the King's Fund.

We each had different motives for wanting to organise a jury, but in discussions both before and after the project, we found that we had many things in common. In this chapter we reflect on our experiences and explore some of the issues surrounding the organisation of citizens' juries within health authorities.

Throughout the project we worked on four different levels:

- the personal level, which includes our personal beliefs and why we wanted to organise a jury;
- the interpersonal level, which includes our relationships with jurors, colleagues and others involved in the project;
- the organisational level, in which we explored the implications of the project for the health authority as an organisation;
- the wider environment, which includes each authority's relationship with the King's Fund, the community health council and other organisations.

This chapter includes discussion about each of these levels and the relationships and occasional tensions between them. In this chapter we examine our reasons for wanting to organise a jury and the role of the steering group and other agencies involved in the process. We look at the impact of the jury on the health authority, and what we learned as a result of this experience. Finally, we offer some thoughts about the future development of citizens' juries in the UK.

Reasons for organising a jury

Each of us relished the challenge of getting involved in a new initiative. We wanted the opportunity to try to put a relatively new idea into practice. Despite our different backgrounds, we shared a commitment to involving local people in decision-making about their health services. For Maureen and Gill, this personal commitment was the principal motive for getting involved in the project.

Although Zoe shared this commitment, her primary motivating factor was different. She was to oversee the implementation of Sir Kenneth Calman and Deirdre Hine's report A *Policy Framework for Commissioning Cancer Services* (London: DoH, 1995) in the East Sussex, Brighton & Hove Health Authority, and was facing some difficult questions. The Calman/Hine report recommends that services be developed to improve outcomes in treatment for people with cancer. The East Sussex, Brighton & Hove Health Authority wanted to address the possible tension between clinical effectiveness and local access to gynaecological services, which were located in a number of hospitals across the area. The authority also wanted to obtain a user perspective and a population perspective on this issue.

Although the subject matter was not the key reason for organising a jury in Sunderland or Buckinghamshire, a great deal of thought was given to what question should be addressed, to ensure that it was about a difficult issue that needed a decision.

Sunderland Health Authority decided to focus on primary care. The age profile of GPs in Sunderland suggested a dramatic increase in those seeking retirement within the next five years, and the recruitment of GPs was proving difficult. The Authority were also keen to explore public perceptions of the evolving role of nurses and pharmacists within primary care. The current emphasis on an NHS led by primary care has meant that it is even more important to ensure that the people of Sunderland receive the best possible primary care. The Authority therefore decided that their jury question should focus on some of the options for the development of primary care in Sunderland.

Another motivating factor behind Sunderland's decision to run a jury was a desire to publicly explore a new initiative in the north east of England. People working in the north feel that new initiatives are piloted almost entirely in the south, and that the good and innovative work in the north is often ignored.

Buckinghamshire Health Authority identified the management of back pain as a key area in its 1996/97 corporate contract. Estimates extrapolated from the Clinical Standards Advisory Group's report on back pain (London: HMSO, 1994) reveal that the NHS costs of back pain in Buckinghamshire are at least £5.5 million. The local medical committee had asked the Authority to look at the effectiveness of back pain services, and the Authority wanted to ensure that the care purchased for back-pain sufferers would give them the maximum benefit and provide the local population with the best value for money. The citizens' jury seemed to offer an appropriate way to ask the public to help weigh up a complex array of evidence, including clinical effectiveness, equity, accessibility, patient views and experience, and public values.

It was important that the question to be addressed by the jury related to the work plan and contracting priorities of the health authority – this was clearly the case in all three health authorities. We found that this made it easier to ensure that considering and implementing the recommendations were a priority within each of the health authorities.

As well as being committed to addressing the issue that the jury was to deliberate, each health authority had a commitment to involve the public in key areas of service planning, evaluation and decision-making. Buckinghamshire in particular has a good reputation for the pioneering work it has done in this area. The health authorities were aware that the questions they wished to address were complex, and needed time for deliberation. We are sure that the degree of importance given to public involvement within a health authority can have an impact on the planning of the jury and the way in which a jury's recommendations are received.

The health authorities also wanted to improve their public image. They felt that participation in a pilot project would enable them to develop more skills in public involvement. Moreover, the 'pilot' label meant that there was less risk involved – if the jury did not go well, it would be regarded as an experiment from which learning could take place. Whether successful or not, each authority saw the jury as a unique process that would offer a very focused way of addressing a particular issue.

The role of the steering group

Each health authority set up a steering group to advise them on the proposed question, agenda, witnesses and other arrangements. Each steering group was chaired by an executive director of the health authority, and included other health authority staff, representatives from the community health council and other key stakeholders. In Sunderland, these included GPs and a pharmacist. In Buckinghamshire, a GP and members of the local Back Pain Association were involved. The East Sussex steering group included a local gynaecologist.

The steering groups were involved to varying degrees in carrying out tasks relating to the planning and organisation of the jury. The steering groups in Sunderland and East Sussex, Brighton & Hove were very active in meetings, particularly in making suggestions about different approaches to issues.

Buckinghamshire Health Authority organised an 'awayday' for the steering group early in the planning process. During that day, members of the steering group had a chance to learn more about citizens' juries, to discuss the issue of back pain and to begin to formulate the question to be put to the jury. We believe that this awayday helped the steering group work effectively together. Members of this group also undertook a number of tasks in preparation for the jury, which in the other two health authorities fell to the project managers. We felt that this extra achievement was in part due to the foundations laid at the awayday.

Another possible reason for the increased involvement of members of this steering group was that staff from Buckinghamshire Health Authority were asked to join the steering group for reasons slightly different from those in Sunderland and East Sussex, Brighton & Hove. Buckinghamshire made a conscious decision to involve some less senior members of staff, with a view to ensuring that their involvement in planning a jury would contribute to their personal development and learning, particularly about public involvement but also about project management and working in partnership with people from organisations outside the health authority.

Health authorities have an obligation to work with other agencies to ensure the best possible health of the local population. As project managers, we felt that the steering group helped us to establish or develop successful long-term relationships with people both within and outside the health authorities – users of services, GPs and consultants, the community health councils, the National Association of Patient Participation Groups and the National Back Pain Association. This has meant that other projects have been easier to put into action.

There are, however, some potential problems with the use of a steering group in the planning of citizens' juries. There are dangers that the group could be seen to be merely endorsing actions by the health authority, or that those with a strong opinion about the issue to be addressed by the jury (whether in or outside the health authority) will use the group to influence the structure of the jury. The selection of steering group members is therefore crucial. Despite these potential problems, though, we feel that the steering group adds a different level of accountability and ownership to the project, which assists in the discussion and implementation of the jury's recommendations. The steering group also helps to guard against bias, or the appearance of bias.

If steering groups are to be used to help to plan citizens' juries, it must be clear where the responsibility of the steering group and of the project manager ends. Three of us believe that it would have been helpful if the responsibility of the project manager had ceased once the jury had taken place and the process had been reviewed. We feel that the responsibility of implementing the jury's recommendations should rest with another member of staff, and, if appropriate, another steering group. Some overlap between these groups might be helpful, but it could be expecting too much of project managers to retain objectivity throughout the planning and running of a jury if they know that they will also be responsible for implementing the jury's recommendations.

Zoe, who was responsible both for project management of the East Sussex, Brighton & Hove jury and for implementing its recommendations, does not agree with this view. She wanted to organise a jury because of her role in reviewing cancer services in the health authority area. She did not feel her objectivity was compromised. Rather, she felt that the jury increased her motivation to improve cancer services.

The role of the King's Fund

Since working on the citizens' juries project, we have spent some time discussing the division of roles between the King's Fund fieldworker and the project managers. In the King's Fund project, the health authorities were given a grant to help them to fund a jury. They were also provided with the services of two jury facilitators and a fieldworker to ensure that learning was shared between the projects. The health authority's responsibility was to plan and organise the jury with the support of this team.

In future, if more juries take place, will there be a need for an organisation external to the health authority to take on the role of the King's Fund? Would it be more appropriate for a health authority to agree on an issue to be addressed, then to commission an external organisation to organise the jury? We have not reached an agreement between us about this, so would be interested to see this model tested. However, we believe that a health authority needs to feel some ownership of the process if it is to take an active part in considering and implementing the jury's recommendations. Responsibility for involving local people cannot be handed over to another agency. There is also a question about whether some health authorities would be prepared to plan a jury without some assistance from an external agency experienced in this area.

In these juries, the involvement of the King's Fund gave some degree of independence to the process. The conditions of the grant required the health authorities to involve other organisations in planning the jury. They also had to involve a member of the health authority, and the health authority had to make a public response to the jury's recommendations. Other organisations such as the community health council felt that the involvement of the King's Fund gave them confidence that the process would have integrity, and that the jury's recommendations would be listened to.

There must be a mechanism for ensuring this integrity in future juries. An accreditation system may provide this function. Without the involvement of an organisation such as the King's Fund, the role of the steering group becomes even more crucial in helping to ensure an unbiased approach to the project.

Relations between the health authorities and the King's Fund were generally constructive. When tensions did emerge, they were often caused by confusion about roles and responsibilities. For this reason, as project managers we advocate spending time to ensure absolute clarity about the different roles and responsibilities of the different agencies and individuals involved, and for each to be committed to these. Jo Lenaghan and Anna Coote have written about these roles in their guidelines on running citizens' juries. (London: IPPR, 1997)

Working with other agencies

We have already noted how the steering group can help to build relationships with people in other agencies. However, the steering group should not be relied on as the sole route of communication with other organisations throughout the planning, running and follow-up of a jury. Other methods of communication are important. We used letters and newsletters to keep people up to date with developments, but are still aware that we did not always communicate in a timely or adequate way. Letters sent between chief executives do not always find their way to the staff who feel their future may be affected by the jury's recommendations. This is a lesson for the future. We need to use our own networks of contacts both in the local area and nationally to ensure that the appropriate agencies and individuals know about the jury and its recommendations.

Each health authority employed an external agency to recruit jurors. This was a condition of the King's Fund grant, to ensure that there was no bias – and no appearance of bias – in the recruitment process. In retrospect, this was not necessarily the most effective way of ensuring integrity in the recruitment process; each authority had concerns about the work of the companies they employed. How jurors are recruited can make or break a jury. We feel it might be more helpful to work more closely with an external organisation, whether this is a university department or a market research company to undertake this task, and to ensure that this organisation fulfils its brief. It would certainly be helpful if someone could produce a precise guide on how to work with a recruitment agency.

As project managers, we felt we had many different levels of accountability. We had our own beliefs and principles. We also felt accountable to the health authority as our employers, to the King's Fund as funders of the project, to local health care organisations because of the possible implications of the project, and to local people. Many health authority staff are used to working with these different levels of accountability, and we did not find this a problem. However, we felt it was important to keep these different communities in mind throughout the project, and to be aware that this might have caused some confusion and concerns for some observers and others involved in the jury.

Running the jury

In *Healthy Debate?*, the evaluation of the King's Fund citizens' juries programme, Shirley McIver has written extensively about how the juries were run (King's Fund, 1998). Anna Coote and Jo Lenaghan (*op. cit.*) have offered practical advice based on their experience of organising a number of juries. We do not feel it would be helpful to duplicate the information here.

We do, however, stress the need to be aware of the importance of operating at four different levels. We had our own personal feelings about the jury, about what was working and what wasn't, and about our own roles. On an interpersonal level, we needed to build appropriate relationships with jurors, observers and witnesses. At an organisational level, we had to represent the health authority and its views to the jurors, the press and others, and to 'manage upwards' within the organisation, to ensure that the health authority as a whole was supporting the jury process and that people understood its importance in seeking the views of a group of local people. It was also important to keep sight of the wider environment within which the jury was taking place, and the health authorities' relationship with the local community, the community health council and the King's Fund, among others.

The jury's recommendations

A report, including the jury's recommendations, was produced at the end of each jury. This was sent to jurors in draft form for their approval before being presented to the health authority for consideration. Each of these reports is a public document and can be obtained from the health authority. The questions posed to each jury and the recommendations they made are given in the Appendices.

How much influence should the jury's recommendations have? It is particularly important that the health authority is clear about this from the early planning stages, and that it is communicated to the steering group and to the jurors. Jurors may make recommendations that could, if implemented, have a significant impact on services. For example, the jury at East Sussex, Brighton & Hove recommended centralisation of the county's cancer services. This would have major implications for women with gynaecological cancer and those providing their care.

We feel that the juries' recommendations should not be binding. There are external variables, such as a change in financial or political priorities or unforeseen circumstances, that could make it impossible to abide by them. Binding recommendations would mean that the views of a small group of citizens are perceived to have more weight than other groups, such as health professionals and users of services. In the King's Fund juries, users, clinicians and others gave evidence to the jurors to help them to reach a series of recommendations, which were subsequently discussed by these groups at various forums.

However, if recommendations are not to be binding, it is vital that the health authority always gives a public response. This will go some way to ensuring that the time and commitment given by jurors to addressing an issue is acknowledged and respected.

Both Sunderland and East Sussex, Brighton & Hove chose to send the jury's recommendations to a variety of groups for consultation. Buckinghamshire did not consult others formally, because they felt that the recommendations were not controversial. Instead, they set up an implementation group, which included two of the jurors, to take the recommendations forward. We wrote this chapter six months after the juries took place, at which time at least some of the recommendations had been implemented and there was active commitment to the implementation of others.

Our view is that the involvement of a citizens' jury within a decision-making process has given the health authorities a stronger sense of legitimacy when they tackle a difficult issue. The jury's input has been seen as legitimising what can be a difficult decision. In Sunderland, the jury's recommendations have been used by the health authority board as a reference point about the views of some well-informed members of the public.

The impact of the jury in the health authority

It was certainly brave of the chief executives of each authority to agree to run a jury. The knowledge that the project would attract media attention, and that they were committed under the terms of the King's Fund grant to make public both the jury's recommendations and the health authority's response, meant that each authority risked jeopardising relations with the local community or with other organisations such as trusts, GPs or community health councils if the jury's recommendations ran counter to existing thinking. We noted that senior members of each health authority were very anxious immediately before the event, but that both executives and non-executives were reassured by the attitude and commitment of the jurors as the process continued.

The juries had considerable impact in each of the health authority boards. Non-executives were particularly excited and inspired by their experience of observing a jury in action, and of meeting with jurors to hear and discuss their recommendations. Non-executives have seen citizens' juries as a way of accessing a different section of public opinion – one that is heard at public meetings. They were interested in the possibilities of involving a group of well-informed local people in decision-making.

Perhaps because of the media attention and the fact that citizens' juries are still a relatively new idea in the UK, there was a great deal of interest in the project among health authority staff at all levels. They were able to identify with jurors in their task. We feel that we should have given them more information. Buckinghamshire and East Sussex, Brighton & Hove Health Authorities ran lunchtime information sessions for staff and other groups, which were extremely well attended. Feedback from health authority staff who were members of the steering group reveals that this has had a very positive effect on morale. The health authorities are therefore looking at ways of increasing the involvement of local people throughout the organisation.

The juries also highlighted the importance of public involvement. Citizens' juries can be seen as a marker – an all-singing, all-dancing piece of work to really involve local people. They give a glimpse of what is possible, given adequate resources. They represent a large step forward from what is often regarded as public involvement but is actually limited consultation – activities such as sending papers to community health councils for comment.

The citizens' jury meant that public representatives such as the community health council could be involved earlier in the process of consultation. This has had a knock-on effect in some of the authorities in which we work – public involvement in a decision or an initiative is now thought of sooner, rather than later. Some people are less fearful of involving the public, having seen what is possible. In short, public involvement has gained in credibility.

Implementing the recommendations

We firmly believe that, in order for jurors to feel confidence in the jury process, their recommendations must be made to a body that can act on them. It is therefore vital that health authorities do not distance themselves from the jury process.

In Sunderland and in Buckinghamshire, we felt that we did not give enough time or thought during the planning stages to how the jury's recommendations might be implemented and who would be responsible for implementing them. This is a lesson for the future.

Should jurors be involved in implementing the recommendations of the jury? In East Sussex, Brighton & Hove and in Buckinghamshire, jurors have been invited to join groups working on implementation. This means that there is another level of accountability, with jurors actually monitoring the implementation of their recommendations. However, there are some concerns that jurors could lose their role as 'informed citizen' as their knowledge of a subject and their relationships with health authority staff develop. If jurors are to be involved at this stage, then, like other consumers, they need training and support to help them to play an active role. In Sunderland, jurors have been invited back to subsequent health authority meetings to receive updates of progress. This is an alternative way to ensure that the health authority remains accountable to jurors for progress, and that jurors can take some continuing interest in and responsibility for monitoring progress or lack of it, and ensuring that the issue is not forgotten in the face of other, conflicting, priorities.

Would we run a jury again?

We would all consider running a jury again. We would be particularly interested in organising a jury to address a highly controversial issue – such as where public debate is often discounted as ill informed. For example, the closure of a local hospital or a local accident and emergency unit. In such an instance, the selection of jurors to reflect adequately the local population would be crucial to the integrity of the project. It is very important that local people hear and consider all sides of the debate, and a citizens' jury offers a good opportunity for this. The issue would have to be one where the health authority was genuinely open to any answer the jury might come up with.

Citizens' juries are not cheap. We would consider using one again only if the issue were significant enough to warrant spending a sizeable amount of public money. The issue of the financing of juries must be resolved – many health authorities would be reluctant to fund the entire costs of a jury, fearing that they would be criticised for not using the money for under-resourced areas of patient care. There is an urgent need for a comparison of the relative costs and outcomes between different models of public involvement and consultation – citizens' juries, public panels, questionnaires and focus group discussions – and methods for involving users. This should be undertaken not with a view to recommending one particular method, or to involving users rather than the general public (or vice versa); but rather in order to make some recommendations about the most appropriate methods for particular issues or situations.

The corporate contract for each health authority now includes a requirement to involve the public (this is a stated national priority for the NHS), yet no resources have been allocated (and ringfenced) for this activity. The Patient Partnership Strategy (NHS Executive, 1996) stresses the importance of involving the public, but does not suggest how this might best be done.

Citizens' juries offer health authorities an opportunity to take a debate into a public forum – unlike a focus group, where discussion is private, and unlike a public meeting, where those attending are often unrepresentative of the general public. If they do this effectively, and answer the question the health authority asks of them, is this not public money well spent?

We should also be interested to see the development of other models for planning juries. Would it be possible for health authorities to have a smaller role in the organisation and still have ownership of the recommendations? Could the organisation of a jury be handed over to another body, and the health authority have a role only in the steering group? We believe that these options are worth exploring.

What did we learn from our experience?

What did we learn? First, the agenda for a jury must be designed so that the jurors can build up their knowledge from day to day. Our belief that ordinary people can tackle a complex subject and come up with clear and realistic recommendations was confirmed. We were delighted that up to 16 people from very varied backgrounds were able to work together so well. Everyone who observed the juries was moved and impressed by the quality of questioning of witnesses and the responsibility with which jurors approached their task.

A citizens' jury offers health professionals and managers an opportunity to improve their communication with local people. Conversely, it gives local people the chance to have a say about an issue that directly affects their community. Citizens' juries are about mutual respect – they work well when jurors, witnesses and organisers respect and value each other's contribution. They empower local people to challenge the beliefs and assumptions of those who have traditionally been seen as powerful – doctors, directors and managers. We recognise that skilled, experienced facilitators are vital to the success of a jury.

Involving citizens and involving users

Our work to involve citizens in decision-making has led us to reflect on when it might be appropriate to work with this group in addition to or instead of users of services.

Why did we choose to pose a question to a group of citizens and not a group of users of services? We felt that the questions the health authorities wished to address were about priorities and not directly about services. Had the questions been solely about services, it might have been more appropriate to ask users for their views. In fact, each authority has also sought the views of service users in reaching a decision about the issue being considered. Each jury also heard evidence from service users or their representatives. It may therefore be a case not of involving users *or* citizens, but of involving users *and* citizens in important decisions that might affect the health of the local community.

In the past, most work to involve local people in decision-making (as opposed to what we would define as consulting local people through the use of surveys etc.) has meant involving users of services, usually to the exclusion of the public as a whole. Many health authorities have found it hard to find ways of involving the public effectively in decisions about services. The public panels used in Somerset and other areas are notable exceptions to this. On the whole, however, health authorities have avoided involving citizens in decision-making, perhaps because they view the general public as incapable of making an effective contribution or because they fear what local people might recommend. Our citizens' juries prove this to be wrong.

Ensuring the integrity of the process

We have some concerns that the goodwill of jurors could be abused if a citizens' jury were run badly. There is a danger that the concept would lose credibility if it were diluted or distorted. We would therefore support the establishment of a national body to develop accreditation, explore the possibility of external funding and offer advice to those interested in organising a jury. We found the Association of Community Health Councils in England and Wales' (ACHCEW) guidelines on citizens' juries very helpful as a checklist. An accreditation process could build on these, alongside the work undertaken by the Institute of Public Policy Research, the Health Services Management Centre and the Institute of Local Government Studies. If a national body were set up to develop an accreditation system, it could help to develop a body of knowledge that could be drawn on by others wishing to organise a jury. It might also be possible to develop an informal learning network of people interested in organising juries and those who have run them in the past.

National discussion and debate are needed if citizens' juries are to develop in the UK.

Chapter 3

Facilitating a citizens' jury: working with 'perfect strangers'

Bob Sang and Stella Davies

Setting the scene

In the previous chapter the project managers for each of the King's Fund juries commented on the vital role of skilled facilitation. The purpose of this chapter is to open the 'box' called facilitation (or 'moderation' – see below) by explaining the basis of our approach and, in some detail, how we put this into practice. In Chapter 4 the jurors share their reflections on the experience of belonging to a facilitated jury and provide considerable justification for the principles we endeavoured to put into practice. Above all, we want to clarify why we worked the way we did. We firmly believe that facilitation of a citizens' jury must be a process that is independent of vested interest and open to explanation, exploration and challenge.

We prepared very thoroughly for this work and reviewed it continuously during each of the pilots, both as a team and with the wider project teams. But nothing could have prepared us for the sheer intensity and fun of the process itself. This was very much due to the jurors themselves, the 45 'perfect strangers' we encountered. Their response, without exception, to taking on the responsibility for a citizens' jury was quite remarkable: remarkable in their openness, constructive approach, sensitivity, rigour and courage. They were indeed 'perfect strangers', randomly identified and coming together for a unique purpose. Regardless of age, gender, and socio-economic and cultural background, they worked together to deliberate and decide on problems of considerable complexity for *their* local health authorities. As one chief executive put it: '*This decision is literally about life and death*'.

So, who are 'we'? 'We' are the facilitation team who supported the citizens' jury process on the pilots, using a model (discussed below) that we had developed with Bec Hanley on the basis of our own practice, the literature and observation of the pioneering work of the Institute of Public Policy Research in the early citizens' juries.[1]

We chose to work together because we are very different – in style, experience, educational background and gender. One of us has a background in the arts and community arts, drama and therapy, working most recently as a 'supporter' with a self-advocacy organisation of people with learning difficulties. The other helped to initiate and develop citizen advocacy in the UK and has a background in science, the public services, community action, higher education, action research and action learning, and in change process facilitation. Our shared values-in-practice are grounded in principles of equity ('fairness'), the mode of adult learning (see next section) and respect for the diversity of the people we work with. Above all, we saw this as an experiment in participatory democracy and, to a certain extent, in community development.

We envisaged that, to be credible and ultimately successful, citizens' juries must reflect a new paradigm of democratic practice:

- They will build on the traditions of *participatory* democracy, not representative democracy – not replacing the latter but complementing it.
- They will provide a forum for *informed dialogue*, not debate and position-taking.
- They will be *consensus-building* rather than based on voting and majority verdicts.
- They will be characterised by *support and challenge*, not question and answer.
- Finally, *diversity and difference of view* will be openly valued and recorded, not acknowledged and then marginalised. Dissent is the essence of consensus in a participatory process – a necessary paradox.

These assumptions had profound implications for roles in the project team and for relationships with the health authorities and their stakeholders. We recognised that we were challenging existing norms and institutionalised relations. Ultimately, our working principles would also affect the process, the witnesses and the jurors. The model we used to address and develop a participatory approach is set out in the next section. In preparing ourselves for this work we noted some important assumptions that would inform our practice as facilitators.

First, we believe that facilitation – like teaching – is inherently dysfunctional if it encourages participants' dependence on the facilitators. In principle, and ultimately in practice, a participatory process does not really require a facilitator (or facilitators). Just as the real success of a teacher occurs when the students (learners) leave them far behind – literally and metaphorically – so it becomes important for jurors to take over their own process. Thus, the challenge for us was to become increasingly redundant in the process; moreover, we hoped that jurors would take their learning back into their communities in a variety of useful ways. Second, we rejected the term 'moderator' to describe our role. Developed originally in the USA, it has deep cultural ambiguity in the UK, smacking of authority and control. Third, we recognised that 'independent' does not mean 'objective' or 'unbiased'. As *independent* facilitators we would be relatively free of vested interest and/or conflicts of interest; but we acknowledged that we carried into the jury process our own feelings, understandings and experiences about the subject matter. These would have to be monitored and checked out as part of our process review – especially with the jurors themselves. Again, good teachers acknowledge their own biases and enable learners to help them (the teachers) to address these in the learning process. Therefore we anticipated that the jurors would have much to teach us. We were not disappointed.

So, what did *we* learn? And how might this be useful in the promulgation and use of citizens' juries and other forms of citizen participation? The answers to these questions form the substance of the following sections, for we believe that learning from the process of jury facilitation offers some insight into the challenges of democratisation that now face our communities, service systems and professional and political institutions.

Framework and working practice

Kurt Lewin[2] once noted that democracy was very hard work and that it had to be learned. Learning active citizenship, the means by which individuals enhance their personal contribution to society for the greater good, often happens by chance in our current experience. A child is killed at an accident 'black spot' and local people decide to join the campaign to ensure that something is done to prevent this happening ever again. Staff volunteer to become 'first-aiders' or health and safety representatives at work and end up taking on wider responsibilities. A letter drops through the door confirming that an individual is required for jury service . . .

Immediately, individuals find themselves redefined in some important ways. While the rest of the community seems to take the process for granted, selected jurors are confronted with the responsibilities of justice, due process, fairness, and so on. '*What will the case be like?*'; '*The other jurors?*'; '*Will I be up to it . . . intellectually and emotionally?*'; '*What about the consequences for my work and my family?*' Every day as our legal jury system operates, hundreds of fellow citizens face their own very personal challenges – before, during and after their jury service: *'Did we really come to the right conclusion in that case?'*; *'Could I have said more at the time . . . was I clear enough in my own mind?'*; *'Did I meet my obligations . . . to a high standard?'* People, 'ordinary citizens', *are* reflective and self-critical. They *are* capable of managing rational and emotional responses to new situations on behalf of and with their fellow citizens. Above all, given the opportunity, they want to learn when faced with the responsibilities of active citizenship.

These assumptions formed the basis of our thinking, and later our practice, when we began to prepare for facilitation of the citizens' jury process. A process of learning and of demonstrable integrity would need to take account of at least four dimensions:

- **Emotional**. Health touches everyone's lives and we knew that there would be emotional content to the process. Individuals engaged with the process in their own time, committed themselves to the task and increasingly to the group, and, at the point of closure, let go. This is a tough personal challenge in itself. Emotion is connected, through self-assurance and growing confidence, to the individual juror's increasing capacity and desire to contribute effectively to the deliberative processes. This dimension was and is the key to understanding the approach we adopted.
- **Rational**. Reason and judgement have a big part to play! Citizens' juries address a great deal of evidence – witness and documentary – in a short period of time. Enabling jurors to recognise the challenge in all its complexity, to deliberate on the options and to decide on the way forward that they wish to recommend was central to their intellectual contributions.
- **Reflective**. By finding the time for personal and group deliberation on the jury's task *and* on the emergent group dynamics; and on the relationship between task and process and the impact this had on individual jurors, we hoped to enhance the learning process for each juror. This reflected our interpretation of the well-known Venn diagram of group dynamics (Fig. 3.1).

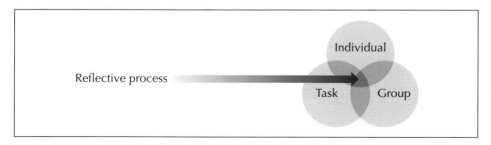

Fig. 3.1 Reflection in deliberation

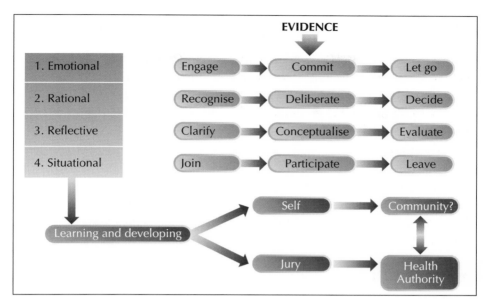

Fig. 3.2 The jury process

By developing the ability to clarify their problem, to conceptualise at a meta level and thus obtain distance from the substance of their challenge, and by evaluating their own progress the jurors learn to move forward.

- **Situational.** The jurors would find themselves in a unique position for a given time. How could we support them in joining, participating in and leaving the process?

Figure 3.2 outlines our framework. It can be seen as a model of adult learning whereby individual jurors actively engage with witnesses in a mature and increasingly informed dialogue. As their grasp of the question and its implications grows, and as the group grows in its capacity to explore differences of opinion and interpretation, so significant personal development occurs. This is about replacing debate (adversarial/didactic) with discourse (collaborative, consensus-building) – without the collusion, avoidance and group-think that characterises careless deliberation. In adult learning the 'tyranny of the majority' is challenged by respect for each individual, the facilitators making sure that unvoiced controversy is revealed and that difference of view or interpretation is given legitimacy by being openly recorded as part of the proceedings.

We were well aware that this model of the jury process and its facilitation was (and is) counter-cultural. Most formal education in the UK is based on a didactic, pedagogic model that places the learner (child) in a subservient position to the teacher (adult/expert). We felt that there was a risk that the dominant cultural model would pertain in the NHS, where much of the evidence would be presented by high status experts (doctors, senior managers) in a top-down mode. Our culture is also heavily influenced by an adversarial judicial system that promulgates a mundane, binary (i.e. right/wrong; yes/no; black/white, etc.) view of the world. Yet, health policy decisions are full of ambiguity and uncertainty and the evidence-base is of highly variable reliability. We needed to develop an approach that enabled each juror to make her or his own sense of this 'mess' through considered, supportive challenge of the evidence and of each other. We discuss these considerations later, in the sections 'The facilitators' roles and contribution' and 'The jurors' experience and learning'.

It is also important to explain our analysis of the immediate context of the jury process and, most importantly, how we hoped that this model of facilitation would lead to continued active citizenship and community development beyond the jury process itself. Our vision of success!

We both work in the field of independent advocacy, primarily with people with long-term needs who are marginalised in our society. Advocacy programmes function independently of the service system and its funders, thus giving voice without fear of conflict of interest or control and direction from service organisations and authorities. For the past 20 years independent advocacy schemes have proliferated across the country (local 'People First' groups, and Survivors Speak Out, Citizen Advocacy and Crisis Advocacy schemes) and, in doing so, have supported the right of every person, no matter how ill or disabled, to participate as valued citizens.

There have been two ever-present threats to this movement. The first is *userism* – defining people primarily by the services they use and the labels (formal and colloquial) attached to them in professional service systems. The second is *absorption* in the procedures and practices of the statutory agencies and service-providing charities that presume ownership of local health and care systems. Both traits are prevalent in today's NHS, risking compromise of the integrity of any process of public involvement.

Independent action and facilitation are based on an assumption of clear boundaries. This creates the basis for a partnership sustained by dialogue, mutual confidence and trust – *not* by commercial undertaking or licence and permission. In the pilot juries the value of this clarification was most evident when jurors worked with witnesses who were users of the services affected by the jury question.

We have elaborated this point because we recognise that the King's Fund juries brought a new dimension to the participating health authorities. If *independent* facilitation was going to be fully tested as a model then, after a great deal of hard work and rigorous development of their question, authority staff had to be prepared to hand it over, unconditionally, to the jurors and facilitators for the duration of the jury process. We knew from our work in advocacy that this would be hard for them. After all, health authorities are accountable in law for the commissioning, contracting and monitoring of the very services that would be the subject of jurors' deliberations. Professionals, managers and non-executive board members all have a clear statutory stake in the jury's question. Others did too: the local community health councils, related service providers, professional bodies, carers and, of course, service users and users' groups. But a citizens' jury is not about managing stakeholding – that, bluntly, is the local health authority's responsibility. It is about participatory democracy: a legitimate, complementary process of engagement for local people – a process that reconnects with the authority's own statutory democratic role at the point of closure of the jury.

In the next section we refer to the issue of *boundaries* and the practicalities inherent in sustaining a process of integrity. Here we emphasise the significance of this theme for the design of the facilitation and the work of the facilitators. For an authority, its staff and its stakeholders, to trust the innovative process enough to let go of a key issue and in so doing to risk their legitimate authority, is a big step. For each jury, senior staff and board members told us of their anxieties and fears concerning this risk. It is to their credit that we experienced virtually no encroachment of boundaries . . . although we did see significant evidence of the emotional struggle that went on. And, usually behind the scenes, the King's Fund project worker (Bec Hanley) together with the local health authority project manager, worked assiduously to prepare the question and the necessary supportive briefing materials for the jury and to put all the essential infrastructure in place (see previous section). Without this work, independent facilitation would not be possible. The role of the independent project worker, initially developed by the Institute of Public Policy Research, is crucial in creating the preconditions for a jury process of integrity. By establishing a relationship between the authority's stakeholder management process and with the preparatory work that supports the jury's administration and facilities, the independent project worker and local project manager can create the 'space' necessary. Clearly, the more contentious the issue the greater the degree of risk to the authority and, from a juror's point of view, the greater the need for a process of integrity protected by clear boundaries.

The authority's project manager and the project fieldworker create the context in which this can happen. They facilitate the context for the jury – one internal and the other external *and independent* – and are the process facilitators' key partners in securing a jury that is credible and legitimate. Thus, a 'map' was needed that both helped the jurors and enabled everyone to see the boundaries of the independent process. From our collaboration with the King's Fund project worker in particular, we developed an overarching structure that could be shared with the jurors to provide them with a map of their journey (Table 3.1).

Table 3.1 The process 'map'

Phase in the process	Timing
A Induction and understanding the question	Preliminary evening and day 1
B Assimilating, clarifying and organising the evidence	Days 2 and 3
C Deliberating, synthesising and preparing for recommendations	Days 3 to 4
D Deciding, handing over and closure	Day 4

Day 4 is quite a day! But the real work to ensure its success is in the preparation – especially designing a credible agenda of witnesses – and in the induction, where the authority visibly and confidently hands the question and the process over to the facilitation team. (See previous chapter and Coote and Lenaghan, op. cit.). How we responded to this and the implications for the jurors are discussed in the following sections.

Key environmental and infrastructural issues

A factor noted by many jurors was the value of good supporting administration, effective communication and a venue that worked well in terms of space, hospitality and accessibility. Here we outline some of the points that contributed to this feedback. Although skilled facilitation can support a deliberative process in most environments, the better the context and infrastructure, the more participants feel valued and the less overt facilitation is required. So we also outline here the practical lessons we learned in creating the best possible conditions for a jury of integrity.

Venue and maintaining boundaries

At one level, a citizens' jury is very much about acknowledging and appreciating the time and effort the jurors put in to the deliberative process.

Perhaps one of the best ways of showing this is in the provisions made for them during the jury. The venues used by the King's Fund pilot citizens' juries were comfortable and clean, with good facilities and a jury room large enough to hold 12–16 jurors without pressure of space. As a great deal of time is spent in the jury room, we thought it was important that people did not feel hemmed in; this could have caused frustration or irritability during a process already pressured by time constraints.

Space also needed to be made for observers, but as facilitators we were very clear about avoiding a 'goldfish bowl' effect which might have made people feel exposed. In order to minimise disruptions to the process, a limited number of observers were allowed each day, and they were introduced to the jurors by the project fieldworker. Another option tried was CCTV in an adjacent room for observers; this can work well (provided there are no technical hitches!).

In addition to the jury room, where the deliberative work took place, we found that a separate room, which became known as 'the jurors' room', was very helpful to the process. This was the jurors' own place where they had lunch and breaks. It provided a safe, reflective space for the jurors when they needed to relax and/or talk through issues with their colleagues. It also gave the jurors' facilitator an opportunity to talk with them about anything that was troubling them and also get feedback about how they felt the process was going. Jurors often came up with ideas and improvements at this time, which were then fed back into the jury process. We were very clear that the juries were a two-way learning process, and the jurors were quick to understand and work with this concept.

The jurors' room was also used to work through some of the process issues surrounding the jury – usually taking place in private at the start of each day. This discussion was not concerned specifically with the deliberative work, but if deliberative issues *are* raised at these times, recording equipment must be in place in the room to avoid the risk of compromising the jury process. This would allay concerns regarding possible manipulation (however unintentional) by facilitators. We also ensured that any flipchart records, relating to the evidence and to the questions that were produced during these unobserved times, were made available.

One of our key concerns was to create spaces where every individual felt comfortable in participating to the degree they wished and in their preferred way. To achieve this we often used small break-out rooms where groups of 4–6 jurors could self-facilitate parts of the deliberative process. For example, this often happened when jurors worked with user witnesses, when privacy discussing an individual's experience was an important issue. The self-facilitation of these groups needs to be stressed here, however, because the sessions are likely to be unobserved and unrecorded – again, we felt that the integrity of the process could be called into question if facilitators were seen to be contributing at these times.

Jurors should have no other contact with observers and witnesses, and the layout of the environment is obviously either a help or a hindrance in maintaining these all-important spatial boundaries. We found that it was easy to overlook the obvious. For example, providing a 'smokers' space outside a main thoroughfare or exit where jurors and observers/witnesses are likely to cross paths or gather regularly could compromise a jury process.

We also learned not to allow witnesses to observe the deliberations until after their own witness slot – this prevented witnesses adapting or altering their cases in the light of previous deliberations or witness evidence. Also, some witnesses felt a sense of injustice at being observed by following speakers – especially if they held different views.

Roles and responsibilities

The use of an independent fieldworker and facilitation team maximises the integrity of a citizens' jury process. In the King's Fund pilot, although we worked very closely with the health authorities, we were very clear about maintaining independence by forming a 'partnership' with clearly differentiated roles and responsibilities, as opposed to a 'team' approach whereby roles and responsibilities would overlap. Clearly, however, our ultimate aim was the same: developing and maintaining a smooth-running and effective jury process of integrity. In order to achieve this, we found that clear roles and responsibilities needed to be decided. In the end, however, all those with a stake have to be prepared to trust the process and respect the boundaries. If they cannot, the jury will remain for them an uncomfortable process throughout. Inevitably, this lack of trust occurred to an extent for certain individuals who observed every jury.

The responsibilities of the project manager, her/his assistants, administrative staff and the fieldworker included: processing and photocopying daily summaries of the jury deliberations (always much appreciated by the jurors); photocopying witness notes and jurors' contributions; greeting witnesses; finding new witnesses as requested by the jurors; working with video/recording equipment; and checking on the adequacy of jurors' refreshments. We found that the jury process worked best when these roles were pre-determined and monitored throughout the process during daily review meetings. This minimised role confusion and supported the jury process and the jurors in a positive and constructive way. Confusion or overlap, especially where there is a risk of conflict of interest, can threaten the smooth running and integrity of the process.

Monitoring of observers

Observers have an important part to play in a citizens' jury because they keep a critical eye on the integrity of the process. However, if observers are present in the room, they need to be monitored in order to minimise any disturbance they cause the jurors. It may seem obvious to say that the jury process is there for the jurors, but it is always possible to lose sight of underlying principles. In the pilot projects, we felt that respect for the jurors' space and process was of paramount importance, and it was for this reason that a member of the project team was given responsibility for briefing the observers and reminding them of these issues, so that disturbance was kept to a minimum. This practice worked well in all cases, but as facilitators we were clear that observers could be politely asked to leave if we felt that jurors were not being given their due respect.

In order to reduce physical disturbance in the jury room, a maximum number of observers was agreed upon with the health authorities prior to the jury, and the project fieldworker introduced the observers to the jurors at the start of every day. Although most jurors felt that they forgot about the observers as they became more involved in the process, we believed it could be distracting to have strangers in close proximity for such an intense period of time. Restricting the number of observers in the room, and introducing them, seemed to prevent any discomfort.

Market research team handover

The role of the market researchers, who recruit the jurors, can extend beyond the recruitment task. Some jurors were often anxious or nervous on their arrival to the citizens' jury on the introductory evening; it is unfamiliar territory to most people. Because their first contact with the process is through the market research company, we found that being greeted on the introductory evening by the individual who recruited them helped to ease the jurors into the process. A familiar face or voice helps people to relax and it helped to break the ice during initial introductions to us as their facilitators. It is at this point of 'handover' that the facilitators begin to appreciate the diversity of the jurors themselves and, crucially, how well the market research team has done in recruiting a jury that reflects the wider adult population that is served by the health authority.

Media involvement

Media involvement is obviously of positive benefit for a citizens' jury process because it raises public awareness of the deliberative issue. However, during the pilots we were also very conscious of protecting the integrity of the process and the jurors while the deliberations were in progress. The media were discouraged from approaching jurors during the four days, but 'media representatives' from the jury were actively encouraged to become involved in any post-jury interviews. Media involvement that took place in the jury room during the process (photography, radio recording, etc.) was allowed only with the jurors' permission and under strict guidelines, which were monitored by the facilitators. The balance between intrusion and sensitivity is often a fine one, which is not recognised by all media folk!

Hospitality

Jurors appreciated being well looked after during the jury process, which can sometimes be a tiring and intense time for individuals. The King's Fund pilots entailed good comfort factors as an additional way of showing appreciation of the jurors' efforts, and we found that having refreshments organised by a professional catering company was less stressful for the team and ultimately much more beneficial for the jurors. It allowed more time for the project team to focus on the day-to-day practical needs of the jury, and meant regular and punctual provision of refreshments for the jurors. Where refreshments were not supplied by professional caterers (to minimise costs) we found that the roles needed to be clearly allocated within the project team to prevent confusion.

The issue of where to serve refreshments arose during every jury; we found that lunch taken in 'the jurors' room' was most effective. It allowed time and space for the jurors to relax and eat; it allowed the process facilitator to spend more time talking with the jurors about their anxieties, concerns and hopes for the jury rather than having to 'patrol' spatial boundaries; and it created a space of warmth and camaraderie where jurors could discuss issues in private with their colleagues. We found that a separate serving area in a communal restaurant threatened the integrity of the process because of the possibility of mixing jurors, observers and witnesses. It also put pressure on jurors to finish their meal quickly so that others involved in the project could eat. These matters may seem trivial but our experience is that they are central to achieving a process that the jurors themselves can trust.

In conclusion

Some of the matters mentioned here may seem marginal, others good sense. The fact is that we found that attention to detail made a great deal of difference to the quality and integrity of the process. Jurors felt valued and supported by an environment that was managed to reflect *their* needs. It conferred a sense that the health authority had both invested meaningfully in the initiative and demonstrated a real awareness of what it means to hand 'their' problem over to a lay jury. Assiduous attention to detail, constant monitoring and effective collaboration by the 'partnership' all contribute to achieving confidence in a friendly and appropriate environment for the citizens' jury.

The facilitators' roles and contribution

The current culture in which we work is often concerned solely with task- and goal-oriented practices that deny or ignore other very human aspects of any process undertaken. It is for this reason that the King's Fund pilots chose a model of facilitation that not only recognised the process elements of the jury but also accepted them as integral to the whole experience – one could not happen successfully without the other (see Fig. 3.2, p.39). Therefore we clearly identified the role of the 'jurors' friend' whose focus was the jurors themselves – individually and as a large, dynamic group. The role of 'chair', or jury facilitator, was also developed explicitly as an evolution of the more usual concept of 'moderator'. This section explores these differing but complementary roles of the facilitation team, emphasising the importance of working with the process in order to develop a citizens' jury of integrity, equity and sensitivity to those participating.

The jurors' facilitator or 'jurors' friend'

Supporting the equity of juror participation

One of the most important areas of debate relating to citizens' juries as an effective method of participative democracy is the notion of equity. Part of the work relating to process is concerned with facilitating a jury where jurors can negotiate and work with a variety of participative methods to enable them to contribute in the most positive way for them. Large groups of strangers can make some people feel anxious, especially when discussing issues that are unfamiliar to them. Confidence is often an issue, and an environment of mutual support between jurors and the facilitation team is essential if less vocal members of the jury are to be encouraged to contribute their valid points in a way that feels comfortable to them. The introductory evening was very much geared towards creating this type of environment with its informal, relaxed and friendly structure. The jurors participated in 'getting to know you' ice-breakers and the room was set out with a circle of chairs – the more formal jury-style tables were to be set out for day 1. Jurors worked in pairs and small groups, and spent part of the time 'brainstorming' together and discovering what they already knew about the issue they were to deliberate upon. As facilitators, we were quick to point out that people knew a great deal more about the subject than they originally believed. This helped to build their confidence and reduced anxiety about feeling ignorant or ill informed. The jurors would learn much more about the issues, but recognising and appreciating their own innate knowledge and common sense was a solid place for them to begin.

During the jury, we were very clear about creating a jury culture of mutual respect for the individuals present, encouraging an appreciation of difference for everyone involved. In the pilots this was achieved very effectively on the morning of day 1 by the jurors themselves, who developed a set of 'guidelines' (the jurors' word) about how they would work together during the four days. These guidelines also usefully reflected some of the concerns and anxieties the jurors were bringing to the process, and created a way to share them and find ways of working through potential difficulties. The fact that the guidelines were developed by the jurors gave them ownership of their process and gave the facilitators further ideas for ways of working that could be negotiated and revised with the jurors during the process. For example, to encourage less vocal members to contribute, jurors were also invited to work in pairs or small groups during deliberative periods and questioning of witnesses. Not only did this encourage equity of participation, it also allowed for a more reflective and thoughtful style of questioning – which added to the depth and integrity of the deliberation. In order to allow for what one juror described as a healthy 'cross-fertilisation of ideas', jurors' name-plates were moved around every day so that pairs and sub-groups were different. These changes were not random, but carried out to support and encourage individuals who might be experiencing marginalisation through, for example, age or gender. It also discouraged groups from coming to fixed decisions too early in the proceedings.

In our politically correct climate it is very easy to give the impression of 'equality' in roles or situations, but not so easy to establish working relationships of genuine and mutual respect that promote a real desire to communicate and work with the tough issues that often arise in such an intensive process. To achieve these aims between the jurors and the facilitation team was of paramount importance to us. We felt it was important to recognise that each juror began from a different point in their development, and that true equity would be best achieved by recognising and valuing these differences rather than trying to treat people as equal. The inherent fairness of encouraging people to participate in their preferred way is something the jurors' facilitator took very seriously, and this was often approached on a one-to-one basis (during breaks and at lunchtime). This was then debriefed by the jury facilitator in order that these insights could be taken into account when monitoring and supporting jurors' participation in the open sessions. We were aware that in large-group practices such as 'spotlighting' particular individuals exemplify the real gender and age discrimination that can take place in such settings, and crude approaches like these reflect the 'tyranny of the majority' which negate a process of true equity.

There has always been general concern in citizens' jury processes about the level of contribution/participation by female jurors, and this was no exception during the King's Fund pilots. The risk of a few male jurors dominating the deliberations was something that we were keen to avoid. We believe that the model of facilitation used in the pilots supported *every* individual's involvement, male and female. For example:

- In all three juries, some women initially expressed their reservations about speaking in the large group. However, in all three the confidence of many of these women developed to such a degree that, by the end of the process, they were willing and able to present jury recommendations to the relevant health authority.

- Facilitators were keen to develop as much juror-led facilitation as possible; on the afternoon of day 4, the role of 'chair' was offered to a juror for the presentation to the health authority. In two out of three juries this role was taken on by a woman, and in the third taken by the youngest and most inexperienced juror.

- In one jury, two of the women who expressed the most anxiety about their contribution to the process became the 'media representatives' of their jury, confident to tackle both newspaper and radio interviews, and resulting in the authority's chief executive commenting enthusiastically on their self-assurance and skill.

- In all three juries, female jurors have been well represented at health authority board meetings following the juries, and several have presented recommendations to the board.

- In one jury, men and women expressed their pride at being able to work so positively in partnership on a women's health issue.

Emotional support and encouragement

The issue of confidence is a common theme during a citizens' jury, and much of the work of the facilitator is concerned with encouraging jurors to feel confident in expressing their thoughts and feelings about the issues presented. It is easy to feel inadequate when confronted by a series of complex presentations by professionals, especially in a culture such as ours where power is predominantly given away to the 'expert'. It is also easy to doubt one's instincts and more common-sense approaches to an issue in the face of this 'expertise'. The jurors' facilitator is aware of these issues and helps to create an atmosphere of mutual support that clearly demonstrates the value of every juror's contribution. This aids the deliberative process by setting up frank dialogue between jurors and witnesses – who often come to respect the thoughtful insights of the jurors and their freshness of vision. A guiding principle was to encourage the 'naive' question and develop 'invisible' facilitation skills that can happen naturally over a coffee or at the end of a deliberative session when a juror is feeling confused or overwhelmed with material. This type of process facilitation is about reflecting back, listening, supporting and believing in people's abilities to work through complex issues when they are lacking in self-confidence or feeling out of their depth.

It is also about developing mutual support and awareness between the jurors themselves. During the juries, less confident jurors were actively encouraged by their peers (*'This jury has given me a chance to come out of my shell'*: juror, Sunderland), and others learned to listen more effectively (*'Thanks for keeping a check on me'*: juror, Sunderland). The guidelines formulated by the jurors were referred to at the beginning of every morning session so that jurors might assess their own effectiveness at working together. This can become an opportunity to air anxieties about the process, preventing personal issues 'spilling out' into the deliberative task, but is more often a time for positive comments (and often surprise) at how well jurors feel they are working together. This is a good way to start the day.

Every juror brings to the citizens' jury their own thoughts, life experiences, memories and feelings about the issue they are to deliberate upon. In the King's Fund pilot juries the facilitation team saw these elements as strengths and were keen to draw on them, while helping to forge these experiences together with the new information jurors would receive during the deliberation. This creates a powerful alchemy of fact, feeling and experience that adds to the richness of the process. Sometimes, however, a juror may be dealing with deliberative material that provokes disturbing memories or distress. The jurors' facilitator must be available at all times to talk through any issues that arise and to offer support (or referral to other appropriate support, if necessary). This requires sensitivity and a willingness to 'visit' emotional spaces with an individual that may not always be comfortable. In the pilot juries, it was often the sessions with user witnesses that proved most powerful, but which also caused the most distress among jurors (and, it must be said, facilitators). We felt the process was about creating an environment in which the emotional and rational dimensions are respected. The complementary roles of facilitation enabled this to happen in a positive and meaningful way for the jurors, which ultimately strengthened the deliberative work itself.

Accountability of the jurors' facilitator

We were very clear that the jurors' facilitator was accountable to the jurors themselves, and answered primarily to their needs and wishes. We therefore managed such issues as boundaries to the process, dealings with observers and witnesses, and responding effectively to pressures that might otherwise have compromised the jury process. Our independence, supported by the King's Fund's own status as an independent foundation, helped to sustain this view of accountability. In some instances we inevitably challenged process assumptions held by health authority staff and observers . . . an ever-present tension for truly independent models of facilitation.

The jurors' liaison

The jurors' facilitator also tended to be responsible for liaising with the health authority if any additional material was requested by the jurors during the process. In one jury, the health authority had compiled a file with extra information for the jurors to use if they so wished. Because the jurors often separated into small groups, one of them suggested that the material be duplicated for each group. This was raised in a review meeting and the authority provided duplicate files, which some jurors also took home overnight for perusal in their own time. This had the further effect of stimulating several jurors to make notes regarding their own perceptions of where the deliberations were during the process. Again, these notes were given to the jurors' facilitator and then copied by the health authority for distribution among the jurors. Material brought in by the jurors themselves covered not only deliberative issues; one juror brought in a list of helpful proverbs as encouragement to her juror colleagues; another brought in a cartoon relating to the issues the jury were working with; and another wrote a poem about the experience of being on a citizens' jury. This material, duly copied by the authority and shared by the jurors, highlights the ownership the jurors came to feel about their jury process. A tangible and positive step towards participative democracy occurs when this process of ownership begins to develop, and individuals start to feel more confident in sharing their creative endeavours, as well as thoughts and reflections, in working towards a common goal.

The jury facilitator (the 'chair')

This role is the more obvious one, usually referred to as the 'moderator'. We explained early in the chapter why we chose not to use this term, and there were (and are) very positive reasons why we see the 'chair' role as integral to the facilitation team and the processes that they support.

For much of the jury the 'chair' sits literally at the focus of the large group process. The role is a high-risk one because it is intended to integrate the substantive work of the jury (the task) with the deliberative process as it evolves through the phases outlined in Table 3.1. It is an enabling role that is facilitative in its outcomes. It is also a high-risk role because, if implemented inappropriately, it can distort the whole process. Therefore, it demands a significant degree of monitoring: by the jurors, by the jurors' facilitator, by the project worker, and through her/him by the authority and its stakeholders. Above all, the role-holder must be self-reflective and self-critical, openly developing a relationship with the jurors that encourages feedback and, where necessary, challenge.

Indeed, the jurors' view of the 'chair' is very much to the point: '*We need to know that you will be fair to each of us and advise us if we are going off track*' (juror, Aylesbury). Managing equity within the deliberative process while providing an occasional 'steer' puts the 'chair' in a very powerful position . . . and an inherently contradictory one. The facilitation team gave this a great deal of thought before and during the pilots. This helped the 'chair' to think through the key process skills needed for implementing the role and the appropriateness of the style required. These key skills are described below.

Enabling the task

The jury's task is, in essence, to produce a response to a predetermined question or set of options that have been prepared by their local health authority. A sub-set of essential work is also predetermined so that this principal task can be achieved:

- handling of documentary evidence and other relevant materials;
- completing all of the witness sessions;
- engaging in activities designed to help clarify the health authority's question or to provide jurors with the conceptual tools they need to clarify and analyse the options and the evidence base.

For example, in one of the pilots the health authority's project manager devised an activity that enabled the jurors to get to grips with the concepts of 'clinical effectiveness' and 'evidence-based medicine'. It was extremely successful in ensuring that the jurors were then able to test very rigorously indeed witness evidence from a variety of contending sources. During such sessions the 'chair's' contribution reduces to a minimum: introduce the contributors, literally move out of the way, support a review of the learning and assist closure of the session.

However, in witness sessions the role can become much more interventionist – especially with witnesses who break the rules! The 'rules' are simple: focus on the jury question, present evidence in a clear way that is free of jargon, do not exceed the allotted time, and engage in a (non-adversarial) question and answer process. The worst abuse of these 'rules' related to poor time-keeping – principally because witnesses were so keen to get *their* material across and to establish *their* position. We found that, by meeting the witnesses just before their allotted time and going through the process with them, and by contributing to the quality check of any material (hand-outs) they had produced, the 'chair' could help to prepare the ground for the most effective witness sessions.

Another factor that contributed to such effectiveness was the facilitation of a non-adversarial form of questioning. To do this we developed an approach based on the principles of action learning, which distinguishes between two kinds of questions: questions of clarification and fact, whereby jurors can complete and/or correct the witnesses' evidence in their own minds; and questions designed to deepen the analysis and enrich the jury's evidence base. The 'chair' helps to achieve this by structuring the questioning process. Jurors are invited to ask the first type of question immediately after they have heard the evidence, then they are given five to ten minutes working in pairs or small groups to *reflect* on what they have heard and to develop one or two considered questions on behalf of the jury as a whole.

Jurors responded very positively to this approach and witnesses began to engage in a supportive, challenging, dialogue in the second part of the questioning process – having had a chance to stop and to reflect in their own time. This process also helped to sustain high levels of energy and to ensure that each witness was approached in a fresh stimulating way rather than in a more mechanical, less engaging manner. Witnesses consistently commented on the high quality of the questioning, and jurors learned to trust each other in building a reliable and rigorous, shared understanding through their use of these sessions. The 'chair's' role was to ensure the balance of support and challenge in the process. This could extend to asking questions on behalf of the jury if it became appropriate, to sharpen the clarification or to resolve misunderstandings. The *independence* of the 'chair' is crucial in this respect; and it raises the interesting question of whether the 'chair' should be knowledgeable in the field of the jury's question (see below).

Time-keeping and pacing

Four days preceded by an introductory evening is a very tight time-frame for a citizens' jury. The jury facilitator has a key time-management responsibility. Each session has its own objectives, each day its purposes – and, of course, the task has to be completed at the appointed (literally) hour when the health authority's chief executive arrives to receive the jury's recommendations.

We found that a citizens' jury has its own rhythm and the 'chair', by monitoring and pacing and managing the time boundaries, can facilitate this to good effect . . . although sometimes this can be quite hair-raising. The early rhythm can falter as the jury finds its feet. This is fine but it has to be tested so that an optimum working rhythm can be found, particularly for the second and third days. The final day is frenetic! Calming the pace early on is crucial; then as the urgency builds, it is important that the jury finds its own rhythms – including extemporisation – as it generates its analysis and recommendations. We noted above that 'badly behaved' witnesses can jeopardise timing; so can an ill-prepared jury facilitator! Sensing the jury's rhythm while noticing individual variations is integral to chairing the process. It means knowing where latitude will help and/or appreciating where firm, authoritative reminders are more appropriate. This requires constant attention and 'subliminal' checking with the jurors' facilitator – a good reason for the facilitation team to sit opposite each other for most of the process. Finally, this aspect of the process facilitation is checked out regularly with the jurors themselves. It is *their* rhythm and any discomfort is usually an indication of deeper process needs. Above all, this ensures that the 'chair' can advise and steer but not direct and control. (See also Chapter 4.)

Recording, monitoring, surfacing and framing

The most powerful tool in the 'chair's' possession is the felt-tip pen! The 'power of the pen' is explored with jurors on the first morning. Judicious use of the pen in recording findings, in checking and monitoring conclusions and in articulating key learning points saves the jurors a great deal of work. And it risks leaving too much to the 'chair'. For example, one jury wanted to redefine the health authority's question as a goal. This is quite a challenging process of synthesis whereby subtle changes in wording could distort the jury's purpose and the direction of deliberation. It is also highly controversial and needed to be recorded openly, clearly and visibly. In another instance, jurors were encouraged to check the 'chair's' summary of their conclusions – they supervised a significant rewrite! Later in the same jury a juror took the pen and engaged with his fellow jurors in clarifying their record. The 'chair' must always be open to such interventions and has continually to elicit feedback on the quality, reliability and accuracy of the draft material produced as a result of the jury's deliberations. Another useful check is provided when the project worker writes up an account of each day's work for validation and use by the jurors. So, 'surfacing' means literally bringing out and making visible the jurors' record of the process, and their productivity too.

'Framing' is another high-risk challenge. Here the 'chair' can use the 'power of the pen' to offer the jurors some models and concepts to aid the deliberating process. 'Framing' in facilitation usually entails unblocking the process when it becomes stalled or misdirected. It involves using relatively simple constructs to help jurors see (literally and metaphorically) their immediate problem. For example, jurors often want to propose an ideal solution to the authority's question but know it won't necessarily work in practice. Moreover, witnesses often propose ideal and biased solutions reflecting their professional interests rather than those of the wider community. The jury's challenge was to perceive the dilemmas this left them. So, the 'chair' framed the problem using the simple models shown in Figs 3.3 and 3.4.

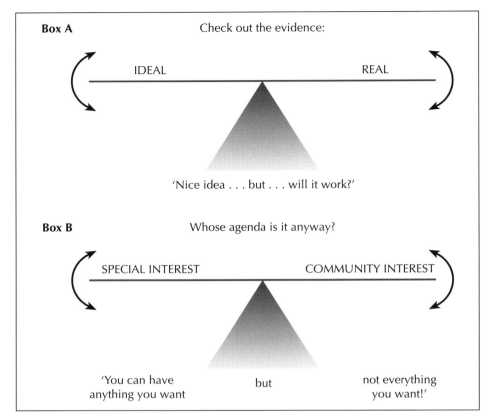

Fig. 3.3 Assessing the evidence

The simple constructs illustrated in Fig. 3.3 can help jurors, if they wish, to untangle substance from style in the witness evidence. Another form of framing facilitated the production of a coherent set of recommendations towards the end of the process:

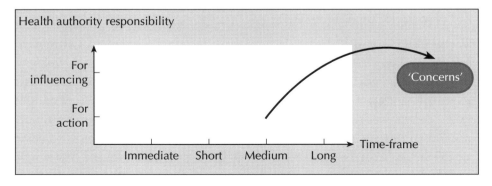

Fig. 3.4 Structuring recommendations

The simple matrix shown in Fig. 3.4 demonstrates the problem faced by public authorities: namely, a great deal that they would like to do is constrained by other agencies and institutions. Consequently, there are limitations on the actions they can take without working on influencing key stakeholders: for example, government or professional bodies. Yet jurors want a lot to happen as a result of their efforts and recognise that blockages need to be overcome.

By identifying, from their learning, areas for influence, the jurors were able to confront this potential ambiguity. The 'Concerns' box was a place to put, explicitly, matters that had to be left unresolved. The framework also helped the jurors to untangle their legitimate worries about matters that needed to be addressed urgently and freed them to build their own vision and sense of the direction that the authority could foster. Two juries created a vision of a better future where there had been none before – an exciting example of how creative this process can be.

Thus, 'framing' can help to release jurors' creativity by offering ways of thinking about the question and addressing the complexity of the evidence without remaining trapped by the content of the deliberative process. The best 'framing' crystallises frameworks from within the jurors' deliberations; the worst uses concepts and structures that already exist in the chosen field of policy in the mistaken belief that 'theory' reflects objective truth. 'Framing' is clearly a high-risk form of the facilitator's art and must be used self-critically and sparingly. Although it does not require expertise in the field (e.g. health policy), an understanding that is sufficient to debunk jargon or demystify new concepts is helpful. Thus, the 'chair's' background knowledge *may* be helpful but it also adds to the risks inherent in the role.

Assuring boundaries and validation

We have noted earlier that 'boundaries' to the process – physical and inter-personal – were critical to the integrity of the deliberation. Although the jurors' facilitator can monitor the informal boundaries that are characteristic of any contentious situation in which public authorities' decisions are opened up to wider scrutiny, the jury facilitator has to manage this aspect of the process very much in the public domain of the formal agenda sessions of the jury. The willingness of the health authority to let go of its issues; the compliance of the witnesses to the agenda and 'ground rules'; the unobtrusiveness of observers; the responsiveness of the project team to new needs (e.g. jurors' requests for additional witnesses) – all influence the integrity of the jury process and their management helps the 'chair' ensure that a transparently independent process is retained. Tensions arise when, for example, witnesses 'steal' time and ignore gentle requests to curtail their contribution, or when health authority staff are visibly uneasy with the direction of a line of questioning. We were sure that such instances could be handled with sensitivity, tact and flexibility and that the most important 'safety check' was to seek validation: primarily from the jurors themselves but also from the reviews of the jury process, chaired by the project fieldworker at the end of each day. Both sources of feedback are critical in helping the 'chair' assess the appropriateness of her or his implementation of the role and in identifying improvements that can be made. There were occasions when the 'chair' had to explain risks that were taken or styles of working that had caused significant discomfort at the time. This is very much in the nature of process learning.

Support and challenge

The notion of 'support and challenge' is central to good facilitation. The 'chair', while providing an open style of enabling the deliberation, must also be free to challenge all germane aspects of the substance of the jury question: the agenda setting, the balance of the witnesses, the witness and documentary evidence, and the management arrangements. This may include requesting additional information for the jurors or asking questions on their behalf if she or he identifies a gap or senses uncertainty or confusion among them. Again, this is risky, and unacceptable if there is no process of validation. There is also support and challenge in the process between the two facilitators. Their mutual reflection and monitoring of each other's performance is critical to ensuring that the 'chair' does not influence or direct the jury. If the jurors' facilitator's primary loyalty is to the jurors themselves, then the 'chair's' primary focus is the integrity of the whole process. This creates a tension within the facilitation team: what if the jurors go off at a tangent or allow one of their number to dominate? What if a witness attracts particular sympathy for their 'case' on the basis of evidence that does not stand up? We found that it was essential to have plenty of time for debriefing . . . including resolving our own conflicts and anxieties!

There is a view that if a juror or jurors go down a new track this is very much the jurors' business. We disagree with this *laissez-faire* approach. The focus must be maintained. The jurors themselves wanted the best possible outcome: they wanted to do their very best for their local communities. So we found that, through support and challenge, we were able to catalyse a rigorous process that was both safe – jurors felt able to ask apparently naive questions –

and demanding – jurors were increasingly capable of confronting difficult and sensitive issues. For example, towards the end of one of the juries a juror insisted that the jury consider her very firm view that one of the recommendations was flawed. There were just a few minutes left before the report back to the health authority's chief executive, but the juror who had initially presented the recommendation in question ensured that her colleague's reservations were recorded and included in the final presentation.

Closure

Each of the 'feedback' presentations was chaired by a juror who took on the role of jury facilitator, thus enabling the facilitation team to begin a process of closure where ownership of the outcomes was clearly with the jury members. Subsequent feedback (informal and from the evaluation) suggests that the jurors valued this very much and were left with a strong sense of their own achievement as a group, and of their personal contribution and development too. Perhaps the most heartening aspect of this was the way in which jurors felt able to give positive feedback to each other about the style and substance of their mutual contributions and personal growth. By the end of each jury, everyone had had the chance to work with everyone else in a mutually supportive and challenging way. We observed that this fostered shared values of rigour and accountability while stimulating a significant degree of individual learning, confidence and skill development in a relatively short period of time. Our view that we were facilitating 'adult learning' certainly seems to have been vindicated.

We were prepared to take and share risks through our facilitation of each day's deliberation – one of us focusing on the jury as a whole and the other on the individuals who constituted its membership. We learned that the risks were worth it – on all sides – but we were also left wondering where the jurors would go next. They had ceased to be strangers – to us and each other at least – and they had become active citizens for a while. Health authority colleagues were genuinely enthused by the quality of the outcomes and by the 'performance' of the jurors themselves. Individuals have been invited to follow up the jury process in a variety of ways. The jurors' next steps will be self-facilitated, but we feel that, through their experience on the jury, they will be more than capable of taking on new challenges – or, with equal validity, returning successfully to their present lives as perfect strangers once more.

The jurors' experience and learning

The process elements of the model used by the King's Fund pilot were concerned with much more than the pure deliberative issues of the citizens' jury. The emotional and situational elements affected each person throughout and the dynamics between individuals (and with the facilitators) had profound implications for the actual outcome. We saw this as positive and actively encouraged a supportive learning environment. The jurors understood that, as facilitators, we would also be learning with them, welcoming their feedback and comments about our methods of working together at any stage – even at crucial deliberative moments. For example, in one jury there was a critical point towards the end of the deliberation where some of the jurors took power for themselves in an open, determined and constructive way. This action, along with the presentation of recommendations that followed, demonstrated the consensus and trust that had built up in the group as a whole.

The critical point turned on two relatively short exchanges, when three members of the jury challenged their 'sounding board' and then the facilitator, who in the role of 'chair' was endeavouring to record one of their recommendations on a flipchart. They needed to ensure that the words represented exactly what they wanted to get across to the health authority. They achieved this openly, constructively and with just a few minutes to go before the deliberative period ended. In addition, one juror – concerned that the jury would be trapped into proposing an unrealistic, ideal model that was contrary to its original objectives – took the pen from the 'chair' and quickly and clearly presented a graphic illustration of their dilemma and the real constraints. The jury was thus able to clarify its *vision* and the final presentation to the health authority was significantly improved.

This story illustrates the real power in a jury process and highlights key aspects of the relationship between the jurors and the facilitators. To have reached a stage where differences can be aired openly and valued as important new information – especially at such a pressured point – demonstrates the growth of the mutual trust and respect needed to support genuine consensus. This was achieved by a group of people who had not degenerated into 'group think' and were able to recognise their own intellectual and emotional struggles and articulate their findings after vigorous deliberation. As one juror put it: '*We each had highs and lows, we ebbed and flowed and, in the end, we came together.*'

In the same jury the men and women jurors worked together on a women's health issue, and described themselves as having developed a 'partnership' with each other based on mutual respect, regard and support. One quite vocal male juror announced his conscious decision to '*shut up and let the women speak more*': he wanted to get a clearer picture of what women themselves felt about the issue.

In other juries, several of the women had voiced, either publicly in the jury or privately to the process facilitator, their concerns about expressing themselves in the jury. Some were uncomfortable about speaking in a group; others lacked confidence about the deliberative issue itself. The support and encouragement they received from their colleagues was immeasurable, and many of the women went on to feed back recommendations to the health authority (at the end of the jury and in future board meetings); others took the chair at the final jury session or became the 'media representative' in radio and newspaper interviews at the end of the process. Their confidence grew out of an environment that encouraged and reflected enabling and supportive methods of working together – everybody mattered and all contributions were received as valid and important. During one jury a woman described a scene around her kitchen table from the night before:

> *I looked round the table at my kids and husband. Everyone was talking and no one was listening to anyone else; not like here when we all listen and take it in turns. I told them we should all be listening to each other, and my husband laughed and said, 'Don't worry, kids; your mum has been doing a citizens' jury . . . she'll be back to normal soon.'*

Another juror expressed his remorse at how he had 'put down' a witness during the process because, he realised, the witness had reminded him of a part of himself that he did not particularly like. Sharing this with the other jurors was a powerful experience and a reminder to the jurors to focus on content as opposed to presentation during witness slots.

A citizens' jury can have a powerful effect on the participants in many more ways than might at first be imagined. It is much more than deliberating on an issue and coming to a set of recommendations at the end of a few days. Many of the jurors have become actively involved in seeing the process continue by attending health authority meetings and speaking at conferences about their experiences.

Working so closely and intensively with a group of people is a profound and growth-promoting experience. It is a 'journey' that happens at quite a pace, reflecting the phases we had identified in our 'adult learning' model of the process. It is clear from jurors' involvement after the actual jury process that, although one part of their journey – the deliberative part – has ended, another is about to begin.

This new journey is about individuals returning to their 'normal' and 'everyday' lifestyles – but with new knowledge and experience. The experience of *active citizenship* is a profound one. In a society where representational democracy often disempowers and disillusions, for individuals to engage in a participative democratic process, where their opinions, ideas and personal contributions are valued and encouraged, can be transforming.

Such personal transformations also raised new questions for us as facilitators. These are posed in the next, final, section.

Conclusion – the future?

We noted earlier, in passing, that we were concerned to address, among other things, the issue of 'dependence'. We now believe that this is central and that it operates at all levels: personal, inter-personal, community, systems and institutional. The jurors' experiences described above make the point. They learned to work in a mutually respectful *inter-dependent way*: with each other, with the facilitators, with the witnesses and with the health authority. Perhaps the most striking evidence of this came from their deliberation with service users: in one case with women with cancer, in another with individuals with long experience of chronic back pain. In both instances these patients described the 'therapeutic' (their word) nature of being able to work with the jurors. The jurors reciprocated, noting that the users' evidence had been crucial in helping them to focus their final conclusions and recommendations.

Figure 3.5 outlines the scope of the challenge for the facilitation team. Could we support a process that achieved decisiveness, sensitivity and integrity, given the complex nature of the task and the inevitable tensions that arise within the local health system? Health authorities have to manage this formally on a daily basis. Could they trust us to work with jurors in a way that enabled them to give up some of this responsibility until a decision was reached?

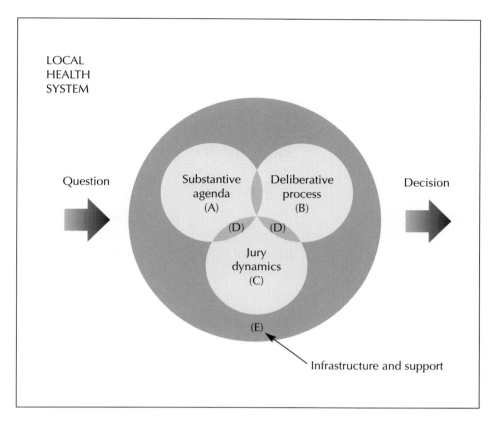

Fig. 3.5 The citizens' jury implementation challenge. **A.** Is it the 'right' issue? **B.** Learning and deciding. **C.** Personal and group responsibilities. **D.** Can we hold it all together? **E.** Is the context appropriate?

We believe that these pilot juries (and those run by the Institute of Public Policy Research) fully justified the risk they took and, in doing so, opened up some exciting new questions.

- Can the 'adult learning' approach be developed for other forms of involvement in public policy decision-making?
- How can local people be encouraged to take up other opportunities for active citizenship for health?
- What have the authorities learned, and how will they change?
- Are other processes and domains open to democratisation in similar ways?
- Should we be facilitating this approach to learning for user advocacy, empowerment and citizenship in other settings, such as education?

This is a rich experiment with implications far wider than the pilots.

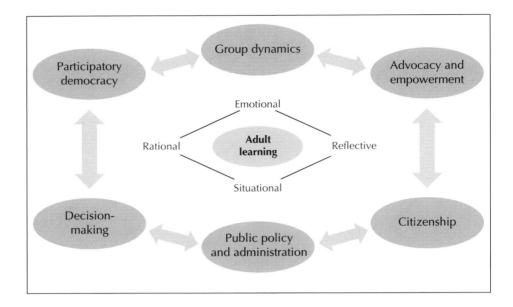

Fig. 3.6 Key themes from the citizens' jury process

Figure 3.6 shows the 'map' we followed on our journey as facilitators. With learning as its 'pole star' we were able to support a process that sustained 45 personal journeys through the three pilot juries. The story of those journeys – the jurors' journeys – is the subject of Chapter 4. It was our privilege to share the experience, during which we learned much from 'perfect strangers'.

References

1   Coote A, Lenaghan J. *Citizens' juries: theory into practice*. London: Institute of Public Policy Research, 1997.
2   Lewin K. The practicality of democracy. In: Murphy G (ed). *Human nature and enduring peace*. Boston (MA): Houghton-Mifflin, 1945.

Chapter 4

'It changes your life': the citizens' jury from the juror's perspective

Stella Davies (jurors' facilitator)

> *'It's like travelling from Scotland to Land's End with lots of stop-offs!'*
>
> (a juror)

Introduction

In September 1997 one of the King's Fund citizens' jury facilitators held a citizens' jury review and reunion for the jurors who had been involved in the three pilot health authority juries earlier in the year. Sixteen jurors from three different juries spent a day looking back over their time and experiences of being on a citizens' jury. Using the 'jury journey' as a metaphor, they unravelled their thoughts, feelings and ideas about their experiences and, perhaps most valuable of all, shared information and insights about the progress of their own recommendations in the relevant health authorities. This chapter is an attempt to bring together the learning and sharing from that day in (as much as possible) the words of the jurors themselves.

For many the journey is far from over. As one juror commented, *'We're here, aren't we!'*

The juror's journey

'It's a mystery tour at the beginning' (a juror)

On the introductory evening of a citizens' jury, 16 complete strangers gather together to embark on an intense and exciting journey, tackling issues that are often unfamiliar to them. But beneath the feeling of surprise, pleasure and excitement at having been recruited lie the self-doubt and anxiety expressed by many of the jurors' at this stage in the proceedings.

'Do I have the right to be here?', one juror asked himself at the beginning of a jury tackling a women's health issue. Others doubted the value of the contributions

they might make. Some remembered feeling 'shock, disbelief and panic' on that first evening as they came to understand the importance of what they had signed up for. A sense of duty and obligation to the other members of their community crept in, while for some the idea that the jury was just going to be 'four exciting days of no stress' disappeared in the face of the task ahead! However, many jurors made it clear that, above all else on that first evening, the fact that everybody was in it together and feeling as uncertain as everyone else, was an enormous source of strength and support. The first step along the journey was made.

The fact that most of the jurors turned up on the morning of day 1 was a great relief to the other jurors! Perhaps it reaffirmed their own sense of wanting to be part of such a process? The ones who got away (known affectionately as 'escapees') were not a source of confidence to the jurors who did take the next step. Luckily these were few in the King's Fund pilots (3 people out of 48), and tended to be individuals who expressed their misgivings about the jury process being a token gesture by the health authority. This was a fear voiced by many of the jurors at this stage.

Several jurors commented on the obvious difficulties in selecting people for a citizens' jury. It was clear to them that some people (e.g. parents at home with children or those in full-time employment) would find it harder than some to give up their time, and this would clearly affect the open and participative aim of the jury process. The support offered in terms of childcare facilities during the juries helped to some degree, but the issue was noted.

Looking back, many of the jurors saw the value of the 'bonding' work on day 1 as a solid foundation for the task ahead, and were impressed by how easily they worked together on the review day. One juror said, 'We wouldn't be working like this today if we hadn't learned how to work together on the juries.' From this bonding came a strength drawn from each of the jurors and a commitment to the task at hand. It also helped to build the confidence of each person ('bringing out the meek') and encouraged input from all the jurors involved. 'I was pleased at the acceptance of ideas', commented one juror. The fact that all input from jurors was welcomed not only seemed to invite a thorough understanding of the issues raised but also brought the group together in a way that deepened the process – of ultimate benefit to the task itself.

During the next three days of the 'jury journey', the jurors experienced a steep learning curve. From what has been expressed, this seems to be a multi-layered and complex process for them, mirroring in many ways the citizens' jury process model developed by the King's Fund team (see Chapter 3).

As well as receiving huge amount of information about the key question ('*It's an education!*'), some jurors felt that the process improved their powers of analysis and perception through their experience of questioning the witnesses and discussing the issues raised in their groups. They felt that they 'changed destination' often during the process, in the light of different witness statements, and found themselves asking if this actually was the right question. At the same time, previous experiences or fantasies about jury service had to be abandoned in the light of this extremely different approach to being a juror. This was no 'bun-fight' in a locked room, with some people dominating and others remaining unheard and unrespected. Quite the contrary.

Jurors also found themselves dealing with powerful feelings, especially when confronted by some of the user witnesses and their experiences. One juror unashamedly described his process as '*an emotional journey*', tinged with '*anger and horror*' at what he had heard. At the same time there was a sense of exhilaration at the journey they were on, and a sense of happiness at being '*part of the team*'. Coming back after a break of a few days during one of the jury processes was described by one juror as '*like meeting old friends*'. Attachments ran deep and the feeling of camaraderie was high.

The last day seemed to pass quickly – too quickly for most people, who felt they did not have enough time to really consolidate their final recommendations. This was a common theme throughout the three pilots.

The excitement and frenzy of the last day was also countered by the sadness of it all ending. With the pride and sense of achievement at having been part of such a valid decision-making process came the sense of loss afterwards. Having gained such knowledge and expertise, many jurors felt they would have liked more follow-up to the process. It had not really ended for them, and many wanted more support and guidance in how to proceed with the health authority if they felt their recommendations were not being acted on in the ways they had hoped. During the review day there seemed to be a great deal of mutual support, encouragement and advice offered between the different juries with regard to this. The three juries had experienced different levels of involvement from their health authorities, and jurors found a new sense of purpose and motivation by sharing their experiences of post-jury processes. Could the King's Fund be more instrumental in supporting the juries after the event? How could their new-found expertise be put to effective use? What about post-jury support for particularly difficult and 'emotive' topics? In effect, these jurors felt that they were 'still here', and, moreover, wanted to be. Being on a citizens' jury has had a powerful effect on their lives in a variety of ways, and in some respects the journey is just beginning.

Being a citizens' juror – the learning

The learning gained from being on a citizens' jury takes many forms, including the personal challenge and benefits, the experience of working together in a group, and the task itself. A vast amount of information is taken in and processed in a relatively short time, with recommendations to make and a deadline to meet.

The journey of the juror

'I will never forget the experience.' (a juror)

From discussions with other jurors, many felt highly privileged and proud to be part of such a process. In a society where, at worst, public involvement is non-existent or, at best, limited (or limiting), the chance to devote a substantial amount of time immersed in discussions of such important and relevant health issues was extremely exciting for the jurors. It is clear that people really do care, are interested and are willing to get involved – all they need is the opportunity and the belief that something is achievable. The jurors who took part risked disappointment. Was it just another public relations exercise? Would their recommendations really be taken seriously? Is the King's Fund doing more to make sure the jury findings go nation-wide? In retrospect, many now feel that the risk was well worth taking, and would do it all again tomorrow if they could!

From the individual perspective, the sense of gaining new knowledge – not just about the key question itself but also about the whole functioning of the Health Service – was considered an important benefit gained. As one juror commented: *'I have more care of health authority issues now, and feel a better person for this.'*

Some felt more confidence in the health authority from their experience, others more cynical; but a sense of the need to change the culture emerged from this. It was a real insight for most, but having become better informed about NHS issues left many jurors with a sense of responsibility towards other, less informed members of their community. People wanted to share their knowledge with friends and family, and some fostered a desire to become more involved in community work generally: '*I would like to contribute more now in community matters – involving young people more, perhaps.*'

The key to this type of involvement seems to stem from a growing confidence in many of the jurors who participated – understanding is not the only power, there is also the desire and confidence to use it. One woman felt the jury work had helped her '*to look outwards – back into the real world*'. She described the experience as '*an education – it encouraged me to use my brain*'. Another expressed his growing confidence to '*take part in community issues and disputes*' since being on the citizens' jury. Another man felt it had encouraged his creativity, channelling it into other relevant areas of life. Although each individual embarked upon his or her own personal journey of growth and development during the four days (and afterwards), the sense of being part of a group, the jury, has stayed with them as an integral and rewarding part of the experience.

The jury as a large group

'*The group developed a powerful intensity, greater than the sum of its parts.*'

(a juror)

When a group of strangers get together to focus on a task, anything can happen. They all bring their own views, experiences, prejudices and ways of being to the open forum, and each then makes adjustments and adaptations according to what is expected of them, how they feel in the situation and in response to the other people around them. Appreciation and respect of difference were elements that the facilitation team were keen to foster, seeing each person as an individual with something unique and special to offer. Working together in a way that encouraged this was the foundation of the process, and, ultimately, of achieving the task.

The learning that was gained by the groups of jurors *and* the facilitators during the citizens' juries was substantial, and inter-connects deeply with the process of each individual. The jurors themselves have expressed this in a variety of ways, recognising the commitment of the group, not just to the task in hand but to each other as well. This open support and encouragement was a major contribution to the development of individual jurors' confidence. The tolerance and respect for other people's views were commented on by many jurors, who learned to feel safe in expressing themselves without fear of being made to feel foolish. Several jurors commented that they learned to listen and many felt they had developed an open-mindedness through sharing and listening to each other's ideas during the process. The level of questioning deepened as the process unfolded, and jurors' abilities to extract the important information from witnesses were encouraged by a group willingness to take risks in their dialogues with professionals – supported by each other.

Coming to a group understanding of a complex issue was very exciting for these jurors, and there was an acknowledgement of the focus and clarity required to keep up the momentum, and to come to conclusions together on the final day, under great time constraints. Working as a team while maintaining one's individual identity and journey in such a pressured and unfamiliar environment is no mean feat but the jurors saw their direction clearly – 'We were working together towards a common goal'.

The task and recommendations

'There's not enough time!' (the jurors)

On the whole, jurors felt satisfied with the result of their combined efforts. Several people commented that the question needed to be re-phrased as the task unfolded and the relevant information came to light. Each witness presented new facts and a new perspective, which required the jurors to stop, appraise and incorporate this fresh element. User witnesses had a profound and powerful effect on the jurors and their ultimate recommendations in two of the pilots. Jurors appreciated the support and guidance of the facilitators in summing up and clarifying where they were in the journey, and many felt that their final recommendations were actually better than the 'tight, subjective' view of the people who had asked them to consider the problem. The sense of achievement, through the sharing of views and final deliberations, was enormous for the people involved.

Some jurors felt that a break in the process of the jury helped them to process the copious amounts of information they had received, whereas others felt a 'run-through' jury helped with group cohesion. It seems that running all the way through with a jury intensifies the experience, but with such an emotive issue as gynaecological cancer, as in the East Sussex jury, it is difficult to make a fair assessment of the timings in this way. Both issues would have tended to make the experience quite intense and demanding.

The jurors had a lot to say about day 4. The consensus is 'not enough time' to really reflect on the recommendations as a whole jury. The general feeling, especially in the East Sussex and Buckinghamshire juries, was of being rushed and not well enough prepared as a group to make recommendations to the health authorities. Jurors would have welcomed time to bring their smaller group recommendations together into something that made more sense to them, and was properly interrelated. As it was, they felt somewhat disconnected from the other groups, and wanted to bring their work together in a more concrete way. The idea of having an extra half day in which to achieve this was whole-heartedly approved by the jurors.

Comments and concerns

'What happens next?' (the jurors)

One of the most successful outcomes of this jurors' review day was the sharing of experiences and ideas about post-jury work connected to the recommendations. Some jurors were pleased to have been involved in recent conferences about citizens' juries, and felt involved and informed by their health authority. Others felt that their health authority was not visibly supporting them with and/or notifying them of changes in connection with the recommendations they had presented. They felt frustrated and irritated by this, and wondered what more they could do to 'get things moving'. There was an acknowledgement that 'things take time', but they felt that short-term recommendations could and should be implemented as soon as possible – and if not, why not? By sharing experiences of contact with health authorities, jurors began to realise that in some cases they were not being kept sufficiently up to date with current proceedings. The potential for ongoing post-jury monitoring by the jurors was raised, and the possibility of involving the King's Fund in this role seemed a viable option. Several jurors talked about meeting in the near future to discuss strategies for dealing with their health authority, with the hope of getting things moving again. The sense of working together and staying deeply involved with the process is still very strong among these jurors, who rightly feel that the effort and time they put in merit action – and they are keen to see it through.

'There is a sense of duty with this now.' (the jurors)

Jurors' comments

'After what seemed a daunting task at the beginning the experience was very enjoyable, and something I would be happy to do again if the opportunity arose. The facilitators helped enormously.'

'We met as strangers, admired the patients' courage, heard the specialists', listened as individuals, discussed as a group, recommended as a team. Thank you for letting me be a part.'

'I was honoured to be a part of the citizens' jury. I found the experience to be informative, interesting, well organised and worthwhile, even though it was quite mentally exhausting.'

'A nerve-racking, exciting and challenging experience, with an exciting timescale. Extremely rewarding in terms of result, achievement and the comradeship developed between the jurors, with the opportunities for continued developmental involvement.'

'After self-doubt and trepidation, being a juror was a profound experience, bringing the awareness of local health service problems and citizens' needs to the fore. Also listening to the opinions of both witnesses and jurors.'

'At first, "Why me?", unsure, apprehensive, daunting; but finally stimulating, very worthwhile, working as part of a team, privileged, helping to develop a people's response, hopefully influencing a better health care service.'

'Was an education, learning more about the NHS in a few days than I'd known in my lifetime. Also respecting other people's point of view, and to compromise when in disagreement.'

'The information given by the experts generates such enthusiasm it is difficult to suppress the feeling of compulsion to use it for the benefit of those in need. The privileged knowledge creates a very valuable resource. You don't just walk away from a citizens' jury – it changes your life.'

'Although the role of a juror was quite a demanding one, it was nevertheless a stimulating and satisfactory experience – one I would have no problem in repeating.'

'Being a juror on a citizens' jury increased my perception of problem analysis and solution selection by group activity. I gained confidence.'

'We need to work together to ensure that recommendations are proceeded with as appropriate to finance and facilities becoming available. Perhaps an annual review of progress with the health authorities would keep issues alive?'

'Intellectually stimulating and fulfilling due to the superb organisation and team effort.'

'The opportunity has further encouraged my involvement and interest in social issues.'

'The citizens' jury and King's Fund still keep rolling round in my head, so here is yet another idea:

K	Keen to participate	F	Finance is a problem
I	Interested in the topic	U	Understanding the possibility
N	Needed the facts	N	Need for a centre of excellence
G	Got the information	D	Dreams can become reality if
S	Short-term improvements		enough people shout.'

Some final thoughts from the jurors to the jurors of the future

'Don't panic!'   'Enjoy the experience'   'Have fun'

'Have an open mind'   'Be prepared to work hard'

'Keep a sense of humour'

'Your own problems will shrink in relation to others'

'What you will learn is valuable – pass it on!'   'It is a serious event'

'Be prepared for a good education'   'You will get out of it what you put in'

'Realise you are acting on behalf of your community'

Chapter 5

Sustaining ordinary wisdom

Bob Sang

> *'Local voices . . . richest meaning'* (Eileen Mashana)[1]

Democracy for health

The purpose of this final chapter is to reflect on the themes of citizenship, participation, decision-making and health policy and to propose some principles for future development and further deliberation. In particular, it addresses the dilemmas of 'governance' thrown up both for the health authorities as publicly accountable bodies and for the jurors as fellow citizens. Chapter 4 richly illustrates the enthusiasm and commitment catalysed by the citizens' juries pilots and we know from this experience that 'ordinary wisdom' works – that fellow citizens, working through the jury process, can get to grips with and address tough health policy decisions and produce recommendations that are useful, relevant and rigorously derived.

Our learning has extended and deepened in a number of ways: we have further explored the philosophical and societal debates about democracy and the goals of democratic processes; we have tested the administrative and management implications of focusing on a particular approach to achieving public involvement in health decision-making; we have articulated and implemented, through independent facilitation, a process of deliberation and learning drawing on the best available evidence; and we have listened to and engaged with some local citizens – 'perfect strangers'– as they have grappled with the meaning and practice of public involvement. We have therefore written this book for a number of audiences: policy makers, academics, teachers, managers, professionals, public representatives (elected and unelected) and local people. Such is the segmentation, even fragmentation, in our society that we often forget that, despite our increasing use of labels – chief executive, doctor, patient, cancer victim and so on – we are all 'fellow citizens' with rights and responsibilities that are societal, local *and* personal. The preceding chapters are different in style and perspective, yet, taken together, they help us to create a very strong sense of what is possible when people with various labels work and learn together on a matter of genuine significance in people's lives and in the public domain.

This final chapter provides an opportunity to step back and consider what has been learned, why it is significant and where this experiment might take us. To prepare the ground, I revisited some of the recent literature on 'public participation' and went back to the health authorities who had worked with us on the pilot citizens' juries and others who had also been engaged in innovative work with and in their local communities. This exploration left me both enthused and troubled: enthused by the openness and commitment of colleagues and their willingness to engage with public participation; troubled by a sense that we have all been tinkering at the edges of a bigger challenge that has not yet surfaced. Can and will anything really change for the better as a result of our efforts and the sincere lively contribution of the jurors? Or, to use John Stewart's phrase,[2] has this been yet another 'innovation in democratic practice' that will be catalogued and filed away?

Clearly, this publication has been developed with an optimistic answer in mind! But it is worth remembering that the citizens' juries initiative was promulgated for good reasons and at a time when the UK's health system, in common with those of other so-called advanced societies, is facing significant threats to its future sustainability. Our initial primary concern was the 'democratic deficit in health'[3] whereby the increasingly sensitive choices faced by health authorities were perceived to be left to administrators and non-elected boards – the 'grey suits' and 'political place people' often referred to by jibing politicians. And the politicians themselves – local and national – continue to be the focus for much democratic concern. Their credibility, and hence much public confidence, are at a relatively low ebb, leading many commentators to call for a strengthening of representative democracy through the use of a range of participatory methods and approaches.[4]

The NHS, which possesses no local representative system of accountability and decision-making, consists of a tiered, managed system that ultimately serves Parliament. It is supplemented by an ever-changing plurality of quasi-representative groups, lobbies, powerful institutions and special-interest organisations. Although public involvement is very much a priority theme for government and promoted as integral to achieving local partnership,[5] the power of decision-making does not seem to have shifted much, if at all. Indeed, as some commentators have recently pointed out, the reforms contained in the recent White Paper, The New NHS: Modern, Dependable, are significantly centralist in their effect.[6]

Local health authorities have a key role in mediating this centralisation of power through their contribution to the governance of local health economies. They also have a public duty of accountability and stewardship of NHS resources – re-emphasised in the White Paper – which brings them into permanent tension with all the local providers and now with the proposed 'primary care groups' to be led by GPs working with principal local stakeholders. To foster partnership in this contentious local context while responding to national imperatives and constraints (e.g. waiting lists) and, in the face of mounting seemingly intractable pressures, to arbitrate between almost impossible choices is a daunting prospect for health authorities. As ordinary citizens we have a responsibility to understand (though not necessarily to go along with) these dilemmas as they are faced by our local health authorities – a democratic responsibility that is explored below.

The sources of this set of dilemmas are worth re-stating in order to give a sense of the challenge and the fact that it will not go away. At their heart lies tension between 'health' and 'economy': how long and how well do we want to live and at what cost? The jurors recognised this fundamental and complex question, and in doing so indicated a way forward. I shall return to their learning at the end of the chapter. Suffice it to say the big questions of health policy were played out during the jury processes:

- *Socio-economic change and demographic trends.* How can structural inequalities (poverty, housing, employment, transport) be mediated in the context of an ageing population? (Particularly pertinent in Sunderland and East Sussex.)
- *Epidemiological patterns and structures of care.* When a growing proportion (towards 70 per cent) of the 'health £' is spent on chronic conditions and disease, and when the pattern of communicable disease is increasingly unpredictable (e.g. HIV/AIDS, Creutzfeld–Jakob disease), how can local and regional services be continuously adapted and developed? (An issue for all the juries!)
- *Scientific advance and technological innovation.* How will the benefits of new knowledge be realised without incurring the prohibitive investment costs of fundamental infrastructural change? (A focus in Buckinghamshire and East Sussex.)
- *Consumerism and active citizenship.* Can (should) authorities facilitate local people in understanding and responding to their rights and needs in relation to health and care and their (potential) responsibilities in facing tough choices between often unpalatable options? (A tension experienced by all jurors, especially when dealing with 'user' witnesses.)

With the jury process we offered a simple dictum – '*You can have anything you want but you cannot have everything you want*' – to help deal with these deep tensions. They are tensions and not opposites, and as such very amenable to the informed deliberative struggle that we all observed. While this was going on, health authority colleagues were facing their own struggle, for the above questions are all too familiar to them – and widely researched. (For example, the new Green Paper on public health[7] and government statistical service reports.)[8] Their challenge was and is 'how?': how to work within local communities and service structures to ensure that these tensions are explored *and* resolved – openly, accountably and with legitimacy.

The juries demonstrated that when the participating authorities were 'stuck', when the underlying tensions surfaced as virtually intractable problems, this innovative democratic process could help them begin to make progress again. By clarifying an appropriate question, and by ensuring a balance of evidence that was fair and sufficient, they enabled public involvement that was constructive and forward thinking. A subsidiary effect was to reassure local stakeholders, both through their involvement in the planning process and as observers, as to the transparency and rigour of the proceedings. Yet all this work left them with an even more familiar tension: that between local autonomy and central governmental authority and control. The longer-term impact of the juries and all the other approaches to public participation is critically dependent on how health authorities interpret and enact their freedoms and duties in relation to this tension. That is, how they perceive their roles, responsibilities and practices in respect to governance and stewardship, and what this means in the longer term for the impact of the public voice – whether it comes from a jury, a survey, a focus group or a consensus conference. And, as a result of this work, are we in a position to define how well they can (should?) address this dilemma?

Above all, this work raises the issue of trust. Failure of the democratic system results in a breakdown of trust – a schism between the reasonable aspirations of local people and the promises and assurances of their political representatives. As the next section demonstrates, health authorities can become caught in the middle of this gap: dealing with suspicion and disappointment on the one hand and centralist anxiety on the other. Anyone who has attempted to facilitate a hospital closure knows all about this! So, in a sense, the citizens' juries become a trust-building exercise. They were not about blame and 'winning and losing'; they engaged local people in sharing the responsibility of the third-party role of informed, responsible stewardship of the public's health resources. As such, the jurors engaged with the health authorities' dilemmas by taking on the conditional responsibility of their wider communities' trust – a trust they sought whole-heartedly to honour.

The health authorities' dilemmas: a 'contract for health'? [9]

For a time the jurors shared responsibility with their statutory health authorities for developing and commissioning the health and care agenda within their local communities. In doing so they provided insight into the risks faced daily by these important bodies.

So what is the nature of this challenge faced by health authorities and is it realistic to expect them to change significantly as a result of the citizens' juries experiment? The rhetoric of the new White Paper indicates that they should; but can they? To understand these questions we also need to analyse the choices faced by health authorities as they continuously struggle to develop their legitimate contribution. Figure 5.1 outlines the set of tensions that are concerned with their source of legitimate authority and the real locus of decision-making power.

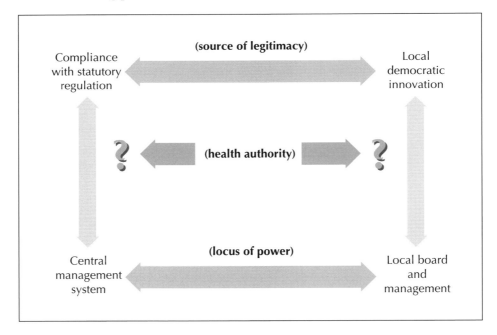

Fig. 5.1 Concurrent tensions in health authority decision-making. The left-hand side reflects the 'old' NHS; the right-hand side the emerging 'ideal' of a more locally owned system.

Health authority managers are used to struggling with these tensions; but their need to demonstrate that positive change can result from public involvement in decision-making processes ensured that they raised critical questions about their style of facilitating participation – internally and externally. In earlier work, my colleague Rick Stern and I identified[10] a range of styles reflecting the degree of health authority engagement with the values and principles of public participation and the scale and scope of the complexity of the challenge. Put another way, the will to democratise health decision-making needs to be matched by a capacity to deliver it.

Figure 5.2 reflects an emerging dilemma facing health authorities: a dilemma that has been intensified by the central requirement of the recent reforms to ensure public involvement in the new structures and processes of the 'modern dependable NHS'. An interesting irony given the tensions noted above (Fig. 5.1)! Indeed, the challenge is further complicated by the dual role of authorities in setting health and care strategies and in ensuring proper stewardship of public resources within each locality. This duality brings their systems of control into tension with their enabling role in negotiating priorities with local stakeholders and through engaging meaningfully with local communities. Setting aside the contribution of the new national

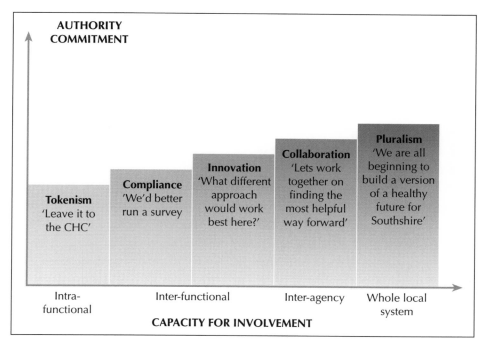

Fig. 5.2 Styles of health authority engagement.

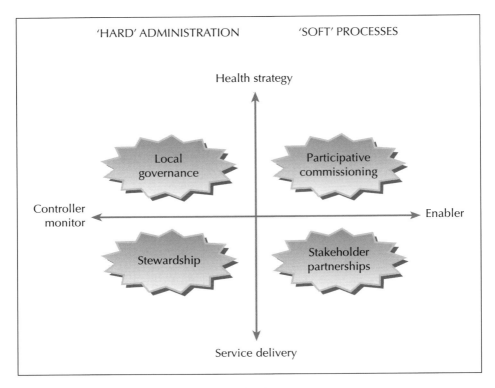

Fig. 5.3 The health authority task and role.

regulatory bodies, such as the National Institute for Clinical Effectiveness, these changes begin to make another set of tensions more explicit – those that increasingly define the work of local health authorities (Fig. 5.3).

This is all about emphasis and, while Fig. 5.3 illustrates the proper scope of a jury in linking the commissioning of services to responsible local governance, it is clear that it present health authorities with a very demanding internal agenda as they contemplate a future with reducing numbers of staff in the context of increasingly powerful national institutions and an evolving mix of primary care groups. Essentially this reflects the final dilemma facing health authorities: will they engage with a *power-based model* of change where they act as the local arbitrators; or will they facilitate a *learning-based approach* that enables stakeholders and local people to get to grips with and share decision-making and the associated risks. The former presumes a *dependent* model of public policy, the latter an *inter-dependent*, process-orientated one requiring a significant cultural change. (This dilemma is explored in the conclusions of this chapter.)

When I revisited the health authorities I found that these dilemmas did exist and that our colleagues were struggling with them as they came to terms with the new reforms. Suffice it to say that their resolution would affect their approach to public participation. Would it be *instrumental*, emphasising the demands of a power-based approach, or would it be *developmental*, encouraging mutual exploration and learning with potential partners in their local health systems? And how was this beginning to affect their relationship with the 'centre': the NHS Executive and the Department of Health . . . would they be touched by local citizens' choices too?

Remember: these are dilemmas, not options! They are uncomfortably expressed in a language that is all too familiar to health authority staff, and largely alien to local people despite the 'spin' given to recent government publications. So, put in plain English, this is all about who decides the future of local health services and how they reach that decision. The implication is that, if things do not change in this respect, we will all have to rely on the 'old' system and let the authorities decide . . . for better or worse. If we want to learn from the experience of the citizens' juries, we have some tough challenges to face. When I explored this within the health authorities and began to focus on their primary dilemma – how to exercise *their* power with legitimacy – they were acutely aware of the ways in which this exercise of statutory authority would be mediated by an growing public expectation and experience of being involved. Ultimately, someone has to decide . . . and be held accountable. Health authority chief executives welcome this responsibility and see it as intrinsic to working in the public's service. The citizens' juries brought the question of how they exercise this public duty into sharp focus:

- *'Are we benevolent autocrats or authoritative catalysts?'*
- *'We may want to facilitate informed participation, but others want a right of veto too!'*
- *'Authorities are inclined to fear radical outcomes, and this raises questions about who is really leading the involvement process and to what end.'*

These reflections illustrate an internal, conscientious struggle about role that is very familiar to senior health authority staff and which, for a time, the jurors shared. I found general agreement that the 'internal market' approach had done much damage by fostering an adversarial contracts management system that was increasingly perceived as a way to impose cuts. More positively, the values of consumerism allied with a devolved, locally identified structure had facilitated a great deal of innovation in public involvement under the 'Local Voices' policy banner.[11]

- 'We are learning to make better decisions, and to make decisions better.'
- 'Local groups are appreciating the difference between being representatives and becoming representative.'
- 'We are beginning to develop a new kind of public service leadership: more facilitative, more open to dialogue, more responsive to the emotional dimension.'
- 'The more we discover we can share, the more we learn to let go.'

This was powerful and compelling evidence of a shift in emphasis of these authorities' interpretation of their role and function: from the administrative mode towards the facilitative. Or from compliance towards pluralism (see Fig. 5.2), through experimentation and innovation. This required no 'road to Damascus' conversion but entailed a careful assessment of what was possible: 'Innovate sensitively!' was one piece of advice. All health authority colleagues recognised that the value of practical experience of public involvement gave them access to a wide range of methods, and that existing relationships and alliances could contribute a great deal:

- 'Make the best of what is available first.'
- 'Good social science research and sound public health studies have their place.'
- 'The community health councils and local medical committees still have a big part to play. It is a question of growing and developing existing relationships.'
- 'Our work with "user" groups has been critical to achieving acceptable, workable outcomes for service development and service improvement.'
- But 'We have to deal with a lot of negatives, too: macho, aggressive posturing by key figures; the consequences of past neglectful decisions; mistrust and fear.'

With limited resources at their disposal and with a sense of others' growing anxieties about the future – cuts, mergers, closures – health authority staff see public involvement as both necessary for sustaining their accountability and high risk because it inevitably affects the relationships that enable them to achieve their goals. A golden rule is to make a realistic assessment of the state of 'local dynamics' before planning to involve the public in sensitive policy discussions and decisions (Fig. 5.4).

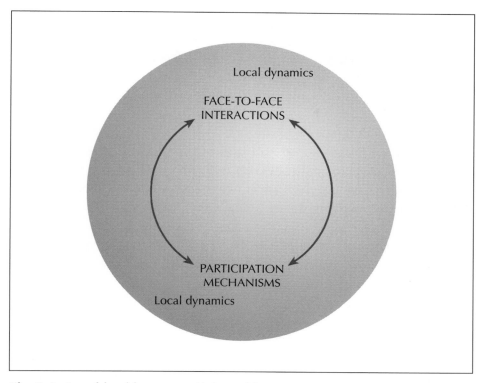

Fig. 5.4   Local health system. (Adapted from W. Isaacs (1992) *The Dialogue Experiment*. MIT Press.)

As one chief executive pointed out:

> *There are no guarantees in this work. Past history, hidden tensions, fear of radical outcomes, all condition individuals' response to a proposed public involvement exercise. So we have to be sure to get the basics right: both in terms of managing relationships and by ensuring that we use our survey work and other methods appropriately.*

In fact, all the authorities found that high-profile processes such as the juries gave them greater legitimacy in extending their involvement of service users and citizens; the problem then became one of positioning their efforts to best effect. We all have much to learn about this; as Fig. 5.2 illustrates, the method of securing involvement might work well but, if the authority's intent is tokenistic or merely compliant, their local credibility will rapidly diminish. Follow-through is also critical, as the jurors found out (see Chapter 4). All the authorities struggled with this 'chicken and egg' problem. If public involvement (by whatever means) was obviously health authority-led, they were clearly obliged to follow the process right through as transparently as possible. But handing ownership over to a jury or other participative process creates ambiguity for the authority, for a time at least. Will they be able to follow through? Can processes be developed that are community-led from the outset to reduce this ambiguity? Someone has to be trusted in all of this!

This sense of ambiguity cannot be fully resolved for the simple, practical reason that things change. It is a matter of trust in the end, and jurors and health authority staff were keen to honour that trust. Ken Jarrold, Chief Executive of Durham Health Commission, is well known for the archive of wisdom on his office wall: two quotations from his wall are very helpful in this respect:

> *'Public involvement is a fundamental non-negotiable and helpful responsibility on a public service. People become responsible by being involved.'*
> David Perez

> *'The NHS is a public organisation owned by the clients and instructed by them to optimise the clients' well-being within the resource constraints that those clients are willing to commit.'*
> Barry Robinson

So, the real dilemma faced by the health authorities related to the end-point of all this work. Would the outcome confirm the process? There had been informed dialogue, listening and responding, consensus building, rigour and transparency; but would the 'clients' instructions and commitment achieve measurable change in line with the jury recommendations? In sum, would the health authorities deliver?

A role for citizenship

So where does this leave *us*, fellow citizens? Why is 'democracy and health' such an important link to make and to explore? The answer is, as I elaborated at the beginning of this chapter, that in our 'advanced' societies we face a fundamental and potentially destructive tension between our health and our economy. Until now some sort of balance has been achieved by ensuring that a sufficient proportion of our growing economic wealth was invested in our health and care systems. Quite what proportion and how best to handle this societal transaction is an ongoing debate. Do we spend enough of our gross domestic product on health? How do we achieve an acceptable/appropriate mix of private sector and public sector provision? And so on. The reminder

'*You can have anything you want, but you cannot have everything you want*' is persistent and uncomfortable for us all. It imposes a responsibility on us to share the health authorities' dilemmas . . . or to avoid them. Do we want to remain happily dependent, leaving others to learn through their continuing involvement in a power-based model of public decision-making? Or do we want to learn from the new starting point – created by the pioneering jurors working maturely and openly with the health authorities?

As Bill New elaborates in Chapter 2, this dilemma has opened up philosophical debates about the nature of democracy and the purposes of democratic processes established to resolve such important tensions. As this chapter shows, these potentially destructive tensions have become increasingly devolved to local public authorities, especially the health authorities, that act both as the conduits of policy and the gatekeepers for resources within the NHS. They have to provide the 'command and control' function for government, and they have to foster local ownership of the outcomes of policy decisions. And now they are struggling with the tension between representative democracy and participatory democracy. It is small wonder that the citizens' juries had to be negotiated and run within tight constraints. In effect, they were advisory: another input to a statutorily defined and regulated system of public accountability. Yet, as we have seen, the authorities that took part in this experiment, and all those who are exploring different means of extending and improving public participation, gained a great deal. They created the opportunity for greater transparency and openness; they become more visibly publicly accountable; and they learned about and reflected on their internal culture and values in relation to public involvement. In sum, this is a story of successful, incremental innovation. As such it is both a grand story to tell . . . and profoundly unsatisfactory.

Yet again we, fellow citizens, have avoided the fundamental questions. We have failed to recognise the depth of the emerging crisis. We have failed to use this opportunity to address some of the fundamental problems of representative democracy. We have failed to address some of the really tough contradictions within the national health economy. We have failed to ask, '*What kind of society do we want to grow old in? What kind of society are we creating for future generations?*' We have let the politicians off the hook and we have left them to avoid the long term – despite the rhetoric of *The New NHS: Modern, Dependable*. The citizens' juries have been a triumph of reason over opportunity! We showed how reasoned and reasonable we can be; and we failed to take the opportunity to follow through the implications for democracy. Fortunately, as Stella Davies shows in Chapter 4, the jurors themselves remain dissatisfied. They want to make sure that there are positive changes as a result of this innovation in democratic practice, and we will all do well to pay attention. 'Thank you!' to the growing numbers of jurors . . . thank you all.

Let me explain this outburst. There is a drug called beta-interferon that can alleviate the symptoms, and even slow the progress, of multiple sclerosis (MS). Until recently, the evidence for its effectiveness was meagre and people with MS were not at all satisfied with the ways in which the drug was being developed and tested. It is also very expensive: an individual course of treatment costs approximately £10,000 a year, and there are 20,000–30,000 people in the UK who might benefit. Up and down the country health authorities have come to different conclusions about the number, if any, of treatments they are prepared to fund. The chief executive of one of the health authorities with which we worked has talked openly on local radio about the struggle his authority faced in coming to a reasonable conclusion. The struggle reflected the deep-seated tension between 'corporate governance', ensuring probity and propriety in the exercise of stewardship of public money, and 'clinical governance', drawing on the best available medical evidence to come to a sustainable judgement about the patients' best interests.

In practice, this has turned into an unsatisfactory compromise with variable implementation across the UK. Access to treatment with beta-interferon is, in effect, determined by the MS patient's choice of home address. But things change. More recently, a pan-European clinical trial of a modified version of beta-interferon has demonstrated that it makes a significant, positive difference to the health of people with MS,[12] significantly arresting the progress of the condition. Now the 20,000–30,000 people seem to have a much stronger case for the expenditure of £10,000 per annum per person. Who can deny them? On what grounds? Similar breakthroughs are anticipated in relation to Alzheimer's disease, HIV/AIDS, and so on. Patients, relatives and carers will want an effective say. The prospect for politicians and health authorities is daunting . . . unless we find new, legitimate ways of addressing such challenges. When faced with the emergence of such alarming and seemingly intractable pressures, our current system looks increasingly fragile – especially when the results of public opinion surveys and other traditional means of gauging legitimacy are deployed.

When people are asked what they want from the NHS, *their* health system, the majority view is very clear.[13] The top four priorities are:

- An accident and emergency service that is fast, flexible and highly accessible – staffed by the best professionals using the latest technology.
- A service that is seamless and proactive in dealing with longer term health problems and chronic conditions.
- A respectfully responsive and caring individualised service.
- A service where tough choices about priorities are taken rationally and fairly.

This is the bottom line. People want a *risk-free* NHS run by experts – 'magic doctors'. What else are people going to ask for if they are put, by means of the chosen methodology, in an unreal, detached 'consumerist' role? Personal choice will rule, and it will rule conditioned by the values of dependence on doctors and medical knowledge and of reasonable freedom of choice. Rational self-interest wins over altruism every time if you set up the process that way. However, the health authorities with whom we worked decided to offer an alternative: to share the risk by building consensus through the active, reflective citizenship of local people. The juries were about options and questions. The jurors discovered that there were no 'magic doctors', just witnesses and evidence whose reliability the jury had to test. There were no 'right' answers, no winners and losers. A direction of travel had to be found based on consensus, not compromise. The jurors represented no one but themselves, and for a time shared the risks inherent in tough choices about health policy. In doing so they demonstrated the difference between *democracy by cacophony* (those who shout loudest get most) and *deliberative democracy* – a process of learning and sharing. Rather than exploit the fear felt by those at risk or pass it on to those best qualified to assuage fear – those who 'know' – they addressed it square on. No one who observed the jury in East Sussex, where women with cancer worked openly and constructively with their fellow citizens, will doubt that there is a better way than the adversarial approach dictated by the 'rules' of representative democracy. Jurors reasoned their way through the evidence, listening and responding with equal sensitivity. Then they, individually and as a body, stepped back and took time to synthesise their conclusions as responsible citizens. And, as we have noted earlier, the women cancer patients remarked how therapeutic they felt the process had been. The openness of the process created a basis for trust, allowing the rational and emotional elements of the issues to be explored. This was the essence of active responsible citizenship.

Systems of public involvement based on representation and/or consultation do not enable this to happen. They may even make things worse by exacerbating fear through leaving differences of view unresolved, no matter how well informed they might be. Public meetings, surveys, focus groups, etc., all have a part to play but, as things stand, all such methods attempt to achieve the 'holy grail' of representativeness. Ultimately, citizens' juries serve the representative system too and they also demonstrate what informed, deliberative participation can contribute. For a while they worked as adult peers of the health authority staff and the expert witnesses, sharing the risks associated with the decisions they faced: creating a vision, finding a way forward that was principled and practical, and noting their concerns. They grew in their legitimacy as they participated. This is the outcome of the adult learning process. As they struggled with the evidence and began to value each individual's different perspective, so they built a consensus and came to a view that both addressed the authority's difficulties in implementing change and reflected their collective sense of responsibility to the wider community in which they lived. For a time they created a live relationship between the authorities and local citizens that was grounded in a growing mutual regard.

Although juries may be too expensive to fund regularly and too sophisticated in their demands on an overstretched system, the method offers some principles of democracy that are more general and more widely useful:

- *The value and use of evidence*. Ordinary people can process and assess a wide range of evidence, including sophisticated and contradictory evidence, and produce their own valid analysis and conclusions. They quickly find out if an evidence-base is inadequate, and know what to ask for to improve their own information sources.
- A *deliberative approach*. Time for reflection and review is a most valuable resource. Providing the right facilities and independent facilitation helps too.
- *Participation* is about learning to learn, and learning to create consensus as things change. It offers a powerful means of enhancing the openness and legitimacy of representative systems . . . if things are seen to change for the better as a result.

With these resources we can, as fellow citizens, contribute much.

Conclusion: establishing mutual legitimacy

When we began this work – under the broad title of 'citizen participation in health' – we had identified a fairly straightforward question:

> 'Could citizens' juries provide a valid and appropriate means of involving 'ordinary people' in local health policy decision-making?'

From our work, the evaluation,[14] and the work of our colleagues at the Institute of Public Policy Research the answer is a resounding 'Yes! . . . but?'. 'Yes' because we learned that randomly recruited fellow citizens can learn to work together to develop a deep appreciation of a complex health policy problem and, beyond that, produce pertinent, constructive recommendations that local health authorities can pursue. 'Yes' because at a number of levels these authorities responded positively to both the process and its formal outcomes. 'Yes' because the jurors themselves gained significantly both in terms of personal development and through acknowledgement of their contribution as active, responsible citizens. 'But' did the juries make a positive sustainable difference – for cancer patients, for communities with under-provisioned primary care services, for people with chronic back pain? Did they set a precedent that can and will become embedded democratic practice? More generally, given what we know about other approaches to public involvement, is 'citizen participation in health' a realistic aspiration?

This chapter discusses three complications that arose as we reflected on and explored the consequences of our attempts to address the 'democratic deficit in health'. The first is one of substance and the potential of processes such as citizens' juries to enable local people to engage with the major policy issues facing the NHS. Secondly, the role, responsibilities and capabilities of health authorities as agents of greater participatory democracy remain ambiguous and only partially tested. Finally, by exploring the health authorities' dilemmas, we came away with more questions about the contribution of active, responsible citizens to representative democracy and participation than when we started!

When I set out to address these complications I suspected that the positive lessons would be confirmed and that a measure of enthusiasm for our collective endeavours would be carried forward. I did not know the extent of the momentum for 'citizen participation', nor could I assess the positive and the countervailing forces that would be stimulating and/or inhibiting greater local participation. What I discovered, and what I believe the citizens' juries have begun to expose, is a set of profoundly contradictory tensions. These are symptomatic of a deeper societal shift that is reasonably well understood but where there is little will to engage. Put grandly: knowledge, innovation and optimism risk being stifled by avoidance of an old contradiction between the elites and institutions of our society and the majority whose interests they purport to represent. In common with other complex and difficult areas of policy – for example, the environment, social security, crime – legitimate (statutory) vested interest is in critical tension with community values and is constantly reinforced by the unresolved tension between central government and local governance. As we came to expect, the jurors had recognised and broken clear of this moribund, almost intractable, set of tensions. In each case they did so by creating, for themselves and for whoever chose to share it, a vision of a better future where none had existed before. Their ordinary wisdoms summed up to a vision of a better, healthier way to live. They took responsibility for the question '*How can things improve round here and how can we achieve this improvement?*' Also, they were not afraid of change and showed no sign of the inherent conservatism that is claimed for the British public.

One of the most telling moments came during a jury when one of the witnesses, a well-known local doctor, was arguing against the case for change. A juror, a retired working-class woman, felt compelled to address him kindly and firmly: '*You see Dr Smith things are just not as they used to be round here. Our families have grown up and moved away. We all have to learn to adapt these days.*' Speaking to this doctor later I found that he was quite shaken. Not because he had been aggressively questioned, quite the contrary – he had been respectfully and rigorously questioned. He was struggling to come to terms with a jury who were not prepared to be dependent or deferential and who had been prepared to envisage a future in which he could find no place for himself.

Each jury was the same: uncluttered and clear; visionary and practical; rigorous and respectful. The jurors related to the expert/professional witnesses in as objective a manner as they could. Where emotion crept in, it was acknowledged and dealt with quietly and constructively. The fear that 'ordinary folk' would be overawed, confused and deferential when faced with expert witnesses and authority figures was entirely dispelled: the jury process, unlike many other methods of public involvement, placed the jurors on an equal footing with the witnesses. In the best sessions they engaged in a process of mutual discovery, taking understanding forward on all sides through an adult-to-adult exchange. Internationally respected doctors came away feeling valued and appropriately challenged. Jurors were intrigued, enthused and intellectually stretched as these exchanges took place and their learning grew.

Discovering common ground and teasing out a shared sense of direction in relation to the complex challenges that are typical of the health sector is a rewarding task. Health authority colleagues who observed the process or who contributed to the witness sessions gained a strong sense of this evolving learning. Here also mutual regard and respect grew, making a nonsense of the 'grey suits' jibe of cynical politicians. The authorities' problem lies with the unresolved dilemmas noted above, but during the juries the basis for a very different relationship between health professionals and authorities and local people began to emerge: a relationship based on inter-dependence that shed the dependent assumptions of the 'old' NHS. This, at a rhetorical level at least, seems highly congruent with the vision of the recent White Paper. Our experience of citizens' juries indicates that we can and must go one step further if the almost intractable challenges of health are to be addressed for the longer term. Indeed, behind the politicians' easy rhetoric about 'rights and responsibilities' in relation the NHS – for example, in the ongoing review of the Patient's Charter[14] – lies a deeper challenge. How can we all work together and learn to clarify, consider and resolve the tough choices about health, *in a way that establishes legitimacy*, both within our communities and across the formal systems of professional and statutory accountability?

Bill New and Rudolf Klein have written about the democratic consequences of the White Paper,[15] and their work elucidates the underlying crisis of politics in our society. That is, they helpfully analyse the disconnection between politics and decision-making in the new NHS. On the ground it seems that disconnection is greater than politicians and the current structures can address. For the reasons noted above, the new government cannot deliver on Tony Blair's famous rallying call to the newly elected MPs: *'The people are the masters now'*. Yet they have begun a process of reform that may begin to break down the institutional conventions and power structures that impair democracy. They may yet be creating a context in which 'innovations in democratic practice' can flourish.

In the NHS this all depends on the new primary care groups of doctors, nurses, local authorities, staff and local people, described in the White Paper, and how well they work. This means that the local leadership offered by GPs in facilitating these groups, in ways that foster a genuine dialogue about health in the community, is critical. It is intended that primary care Groups will evolve to a point where they both take direct responsibility for much of local service provision and, working collaboratively with health authorities and other agencies, plan and commission the range of services that meet wider community needs. The risks are enormous. Will they have the will, insight and competence to facilitate community involvement and consensus building based on informed, evidence-based deliberation? Will they work with health authorities and other agencies, including local government, to clarify and explore options and priorities? And will they have the time and energy to change in ways that will be reciprocated by local people? The tension between high ambition and resource-constrained reality is fundamental. The mutual attainment of legitimacy between health professionals, public authorities and local people will be a long-term challenge.

'Do not confuse deference with an unwillingness to learn', was one powerful message from the citizens' juries.

I have in my mind a picture of a huge mass of people – all sorts, professionals, patients, managers – heading in one direction. From the centre of this crowd a happy voice is saying: *'Whoever got us this far certainly knew what they were doing.'* But, right at the head of the phalanx, the leader has paused to look over the cliff edge that now confronts him.[16] We now know that the NHS is heading towards its own cliff. 1998 is its fiftieth anniversary – an anniversary built on the presumption of a 'sickness service' that depends on experts to find the cures. The search for a fresh basis for a health system that is both proactive and responsive in relation to the people's health, operating in the context of a national health-promoting strategy, is one of the key tests of modern democracy. Our institutions of representative democracy are struggling with this precisely because they have taken for granted local people and their willingness to participate in this search. The opponents of participatory democracy see only apathy and resistance in our local communities. They miss the point. These provide the best reasons to try out democratic processes such as citizens' juries.

As new challenges to health emerge, the potential for mess, confusion and conflict is considerable. The time for reflection, active participation and local consensus-building is arriving. Given the importance that we attach to health, fellow citizens, it seems that this is our time and we cannot avoid it. If we do, we will not welcome the consequences. It is time to acknowledge and grow the juror in each of us.

References and notes

1   Eileen Mashana is a South African community development worker who provided Ken Jarrold (see Acknowledgements) with this statement, which says it all.

2   Stewart J. *Innovations in democratic practice.* London: Local Government Management Board, 1996.

3   See Liz Cooper et al., *Voices off: the democratic deficit in health.* London: Institute of Public Policy Research, 1996.

4   Stewart J. *Further innovations in democratic practice.* London: Local Government Management Board, 1997.

5   NHS Executive. *Partnership with patients.* London: HMSO, 1996.

6   *The new NHS: modern, dependable.* London: Stationery Office, 1997.

7   *Our Healthier Nation.* London: Stationery Office, 1998.

8   Charlton J, Murphy M. *The health of adult Britain.* Stationery Office, 1997.

9   Under the new White Paper it is proposed that health authorities broker and monitor a 'Health Improvement Programme' by working in partnership with local GPs, service providers, patients' groups and local authorities. This 'contract' will replace the quasi-commercial competitive processes of the internal market.

10 Stern R, Sang B. *Achieving effective involvement in local health commissioning.* Salomons Centre, 1996.

11 'Local Voices' was the first initiative in this field aimed specifically at health authorities: NHS Executive policy guidance, 1994.

12 See *Health Service Journal* report, 19/02/98.

13 I am grateful to Barbara Stocking of the NHS Executive for this clarification (see Acknowledgements).

14 See C. Farrell et al., *The Patient's Charter. Past and future.* King's Fund, 1998.

15 New B, Klein R. *Two cheers for NHS democracy.* London: King's Fund, 1998.

16 My thanks to the Australian cartoonist Tony Richardson for this insight and for his commitment to the democratic improvement of whole systems.

Research sources

I hope that all those who helped with the research and writing of this chapter find it both affirming and challenging.

First, the team; Susan Elizabeth, Bec Hanley, Bill New and Stella Davies.

Second, the other team; Maureen Dale, Gill Needham and Zoe Nicholson (see Chapter 3).

Third, health authority colleagues who constantly demonstrate that they are open to challenge and new ideas in this most difficult area: Julie Wells (Buckinghamshire), Mike Shepherd and Pam Charlwood (Avon); Kate Money and Alan Brown (and the learning set) East Sussex; Clare Dodgson

(Sunderland), Ken Jarrold (Durham); Jude Williams and Steve Wibberly (East London and City).

Fourth, Barbara Stocking and Val Billingham at the NHS Executive, especially for their commitment to the 'partnership' approach. And to Sandra Dodgson at the Development Unit for supporting important earlier work.

Fifth, Rick Stern and Sally Fraser (and the Focus Group) at the Salomons Centre. Sixth, our colleagues at the IPPR – Clare Delap, Jo Lenaghan and Anna Coote; and Jim Gobert and Albert Weale of Essex University for their continuing interest and stimulating support.

Finally, the ordinarily wise citizens' jurors, the real pioneers in our search for a healthier democracy.

Sunderland Health Authority Citizens' Jury: Report

1. Background

1.1. What is a citizens' jury?

A citizens' jury is a new way to involve the public in decisions that affect them in their local communities. Small groups of people are selected at random to reflect the local population. They meet over a period of four days to deliberate upon a policy question. They are informed about the issue, hear evidence from witnesses and cross-examine them, then discuss the matter among themselves and reach a decision. A jury's decision is not binding, but it must be responded to publicly and taken into account in the decision-making process of the organisation that sponsors it.

1.2. The King's Fund citizens' juries programme

In 1996 the King's Fund, an independent health charity based in London, launched a major grants initiative to examine the role of citizens' juries as a tool to involve local people in decision-making about health care. Sunderland Health Authority was one of three health authorities to be awarded a grant to organise a citizens' jury. In addition, the Health Services Management Centre at the University of Birmingham was commissioned to evaluate this work.

1.3. Background to the question

Sunderland has had low levels of primary care for some time. This is related to the level of disadvantage in the area. There is an above average number of small and single-handed GP practices, and the age profile of GPs suggests a dramatic increase in those seeking retirement within the next five years. Recruitment of GPs is also proving difficult. The current emphasis on a primary care-led NHS and the shift of care from secondary to primary care mean that it has become even more important to ensure that the people of Sunderland receive the best possible primary care. The Health Authority therefore decided to focus their jury question on some of the options for the development of primary care in Sunderland.

1.4. Planning the jury

The Health Authority set up a steering group of local people to help to plan the jury. This consisted of representatives from social services, the community health council, GPs, a pharmacist, staff from the Health Authority and a fieldworker from the King's Fund. (A list of steering group members was attached to the original report as appendix one.) The King's Fund also supplied two facilitators for the jury: Stella Davies and Bob Sang.

Sixteen jurors were recruited to represent the population of Sunderland. Health Facts, a local market research company, used a random selection from the electoral register to write to 1,000 people asking for expressions of interest. Health Facts also led two focus groups to check that the question to be put to the jury was understandable, and that the agenda seemed fair and unbiased. (A breakdown of the jury members was attached to the original report as appendix two.)

2. The question

The question the jury was asked to consider was:
A number of services are currently available from GPs. Would local people accept some of these services from any of the following:

- a nurse practitioner?
- a pharmacist?
- another doctor?

The jury met for an introductory evening on 20 January, and then for four days on 25, 26, 29 and 30 January 1997.

3. The evidence

3.1. Introductory evening

Jurors were welcomed by Clare Dodgson, the Chief Executive of Sunderland Health Authority, and were given a background to the Health Authority and to the question. They then spent some time getting to know each other and the facilitators.

3.2. Day 1 – setting the scene

During day 1 jurors agreed a contract with each other and outlined their objectives. In the afternoon they heard from two witnesses who gave them some background to the question. Ros Eve, Director of the Framework Approach to Care Throughout Sheffield (FACTS) project gave a national perspective on the question. She argued that there are two broad problems: it is becoming more difficult to recruit and retain GPs; and there is increased demand on GPs services. She gave some possible reasons for this. She also talked about the changing role of the GP and the development of the nurse's role in primary care.

Colin Waine, Director of Primary Care at Sunderland Health Authority, offered a local perspective on the question. He talked about the importance of the generalist's role in medicine, and how the roles of the nurse practitioner and the pharmacist could be extended to offer a better primary care in Sunderland. He pointed out that the average list size of patients for GPs nationally is 1,800, whereas in Sunderland it is 2,200. Sunderland is currently nine GPs short of its recommended quota.

3.3. Day two – further scene setting

On day 2, jurors heard from four witnesses. Mike Ashcroft, Chair of the National Association of Patient Participation Groups offered a patient's perspective on the question. He stressed the importance of partnerships between patients and professionals and of education at all levels. Gerry McBride, a local GP, talked about the role of the GP, the special difficulties faced by GP, and the recent and expected changes affecting GPs. Gerry also explained how GPs are paid.

3.4. Option one – another doctor

Jurors heard from two witnesses, one speaking in favour of and one against the employment of salaried GPs. Chris Drinkwater, a salaried GP in Newcastle, outlined some of the advantages of a salaried GP service. He argued that salaried GPs can focus on a local area through a resource centre, rather than on their own business. Being salaried enables a young GP to gain experience in a supported environment.

Brian Posner, a retired local GP and secretary of the local medical committee, argued that salaried GPs could not offer the same continuity, knowledge or commitment that independent contractors offer, and that they would not have the same incentive to keep up to date with new developments in primary care.

He pointed out that a recent local medical committee survey showed a shortage of 33 GPs in Sunderland.

3.5. Option two – extending the role of the pharmacist

On day 3, jurors heard from two witnesses who spoke about extending the role of the pharmacist. Alan Tweedie, a pharmacist from Newcastle, spoke in favour of this. He described the services a pharmacist currently offers and the additional services that could be developed. These included repeat dispensing services, widened domiciliary services, advice to medical practices and screening services. He reported that there are plans to offer more private consulting rooms within pharmacies.

Reve Atkinson, pharmaceutical adviser to Sunderland Health Authority, spoke against extending the role. He stressed that this was not his personal view, but that it is a view expressed by many pharmacists, who feel they are busy enough. He argued that, because of the growing elderly population and range of more complex medication, pharmacists should concentrate on improving the services they offer now and adopt an evolutionary rather than a revolutionary approach to the development of their role.

3.6. Option three – the nurse practitioner

Jurors heard evidence from two witnesses on the role of the nurse practitioner. Jacqui Henderson, a nurse practitioner and manager at Priority Healthcare Wearside, supported this development. She described the role of nurse practitioners and research evaluating their work in the primary health care team. She argued that nurse practitioners see patients who have poor access to primary care services and that they spend more time with their patients. They can relieve the overload experienced by GPs but do not aspire to be doctors. There are three nurse practitioners working in projects in Sunderland and four in GP practices. Some of these are still training.

Pam Wortley, a local GP, spoke against the development of nurse practitioners in Sunderland. She argued that the options being put forward to the citizens' jury did not address the problem in general practice in Sunderland and that nurse practitioners would not reduce the GPs' workload. There are major concerns about the training, lack of a recognised national qualification and accountability of the nurse practitioner. If the majority of GPs had skilled practice nurses, they would not need nurse practitioners.

4. Considering the evidence

4.1. Additional witnesses

Jurors heard from Dennis Cunningham, Chairman of Sunderland Community Health Council, about the council's view of the question. On day 4 they heard from two additional witnesses they had decided to call to help them reach a verdict. The first of these, Margaret Willis, is a retired health promotion manager. The jury called her to discuss the issue of patient education. She emphasised the importance of the role of the GP in health education and of planning a strategy to encourage people to change their behaviour. The use of GPs to increase patients' awareness of the range of primary care services was felt to be of major importance.

The second additional witness called by the jury was Brian Hedley, Director of Finance at Sunderland Health Authority. He explained the limitations placed on the Health Authority that prevent them offering financial incentives to GPs to encourage them to come to Sunderland. He also clarified that Sunderland needs a further nine or ten GPs to meet the present establishment.

Jurors then deliberated on the evidence they had heard with the help of four people whose role was to clarify any outstanding queries and to help the jurors reach a conclusion. Pam Venning from the Department of General Practice at Manchester University advised on the role of nurse practitioners; Arvind Deshmuk, Professor of Clinical Pharmacy at Sunderland University, advised on the pharmacist's role; Roger Thornham, a GP in Norton, advised on the GP's role; and Joe Corkill, Vice-Chair of the National Association of Patient Participation Groups advised on the patient's perspective.

4.2. The key issues

Jurors identified the following key issues from four perspectives:

Key issues – patients

- The quality of service as perceived by the patient.
- Patient participation in decision-making.
- Patient education.
- Salaried doctors would be acceptable.
- Independent pharmacies have an important role.
- There is a high risk factor surrounding the nurse practitioner.

Key issues – nurse practitioners

- Should the nurse practitioner replace the GP?
- The nurse practitioner can prescribe a limited number of drugs and treatments.
- Should the nurse practitioner work in a primary care team and alone?
- Courses for nurse practitioners are fairly well established.
- Who should fund nurse practitioners?
- They are becoming more accepted by other nurses.

Key issues – GPs

- GPs are retiring early because of stress and workload.
- There are no short-term solutions to many of the constraints.
- In the long term, it is important to look at the introduction of salaried GPs and to increase training opportunities for GPs.
- There should be more training practices and more opportunities for existing GPs to study for higher education qualifications.
- The possibility of introducing a part-time job-start scheme should be explored.

Key issues – pharmacists

- The public already has confidence in the pharmacist.
- Should the dispensing of prescriptions be channelled to health centre pharmacies?
- Pharmacists can ensure that the drugs prescribed are the most appropriate available, i.e. cost effective, best on the market, etc.
- A pharmacist could look at repeat prescriptions to ensure that there are no long-term problems and that they do not conflict/react with other medication.
- It is important to agree protocols with local GPs.

5. Jurors' recommendations

At the end of day 4, jurors made a series of recommendations to Sunderland Health Authority.

5.1. Recommendations for action by Sunderland Health Authority

- To raise public awareness of the full potential of all of the primary care team.
- To continue to develop the nurse practitioner pilots only as an enhancement to the primary care team (i.e. the nurse practitioner should not work alone), while continuing to develop primary care nursing in GP practices.

Jurors were concerned about the lack of nationally agreed standards for nurse practitioners within primary care. They stressed the importance of nurse practitioners being accountable to the GP.

- To extend the pharmacist's accepted role to enhancing drug advice to GPs and monitoring the appropriateness of repeat prescriptions, but not diagnosis and initial prescription. Also to encourage the development of confidential consulting facilities in pharmacies. Jurors felt that savings made through more effective prescribing could finance some of these improvements, as they have elsewhere. Jurors did not feel it was appropriate for pharmacists to offer screening facilities, as they felt this could be more appropriately offered within a GP practice.
- To explore models for employing salaried doctors, as in other areas (particularly Durham), in preparation for the implementation of the new legislation. Jurors stressed the importance of 24-hour, 7-day cover.
- To establish a process for working with GPs to take each of the above recommendations forward, noting that the citizens' jury report asks doctors have an open mind to the changes proposed within this report.

5.2. Recommendations for work with the local medical committee (LMC), GP groups and individual GPs

Jurors recognised that any initiatives regarding recruitment and retention of GPs need to be undertaken in partnership with the LMC, GP groups and individual GPs. They therefore recommended the Health Authority work with them on the following.

Recruitment

- To extend the number of training practices.
- To implement a part-time job-start scheme (as in Durham).
- To explore non-NHS sources of investment; for example, development agency funding, to develop premises, information technology and other improvements.
- To promote Sunderland and the quality of its primary care to medical schools, using prospectuses, etc.

Stress/retirement

- To improve consultation and communication between GPs and secondary care.

Patient education

Jurors were concerned that there had been a shift in focus from secondary care to primary care, but that resources had not adequately followed this movement. They were also concerned that little effort had been made nationally to communicate changes in primary care services to the public. They therefore made the following recommendations regarding patient education.

- To develop more patient participation groups.
- To network with workplaces, community groups and organisations, particularly with vulnerable people – especially unemployed people – and schools. Jurors were concerned that health education should be extended within schools.

5.3. Recommendations to Sunderland Health Authority to progress nationally

- To enable incentives to be given to GPs to move to deprived areas and areas with a high doctor/patient ratio.
- To make industrial development incentives available to primary care (buildings, new technology etc.).

6. Jurors' views of the process and the issue

The Health Services Management Centre issued a questionnaire to assess jurors' views at the beginning and end of the jury. Fifteen jurors felt that information was presented in a fair and balanced way (one did not answer the question). All jurors welcomed the opportunity to work in small groups. (A summary of the results was attached to the original report as appendix three; facilitators' comments as appendix four.)

7. Next steps

This report was presented to a public meeting of Sunderland Health Authority on 26 February 1997, when jurors commented on their recommendations and on the jury as a whole. The Authority made an initial response to the jurors and to this report at that meeting.

8. Further information

A transcript of the jury, copies of the agenda and all handouts given to jurors are available from the project manager, Maureen Dale at Sunderland Health Authority, Durham Road, Sunderland SR3 4AF.

East Sussex, Brighton & Hove Health Authority Citizens' Jury: Report

1. Background

1.1. What is a citizens' jury?

A citizens' jury is a new way to involve the public in decisions that affect them in their local communities. Small groups of people are selected at random to reflect the local population. They meet over a period of four days to deliberate upon a question. They are informed about the issue, hear evidence from witnesses and cross-examine them, then discuss the matter among themselves and reach a decision or set of recommendations. A jury's decision is not binding, but it must be responded to publicly and taken into account in the decision-making process of the organisation that sponsors it.

1.2. The King's Fund citizens' juries programme

In 1996 the King's Fund, an independent health charity based in London, launched a major grants initiative to examine the role of citizens' juries as a tool to involve local people in decision-making about health care. East Sussex, Brighton & Hove Health Authority was one of three health authorities to be awarded a grant to organise a citizens' jury. In addition, the Health Services Management Centre at the University of Birmingham was commissioned to evaluate this work.

1.3. Background to the question

The Calman/Hine report on cancer services recommends that services should be developed in order to improve outcomes in treatment for people with cancer. The Health Authority was concerned to address the possible tension between clinical effectiveness and local access to gynaecological cancer services. They wanted to seek public views on a complex issue that required deliberation and debate.

1.4. Planning the jury

The Health Authority set up a steering group of local people to help to plan the jury. This consisted of representatives from the community health councils, local trusts, Health Authority staff and a fieldworker from the King's Fund. (A list of steering group members was attached to the original report as appendix one.) The King's Fund also supplied two facilitators for the jury, Stella Davies and Bob Sang. Sixteen jurors were recruited to represent the population of East Sussex, Brighton & Hove. Fourteen of these took part in the jury. Intermarket, a local market research company, undertook the recruitment using a combination of methods. Intermarket also led two focus groups to check that the question to be put to the jury was understandable, and that the agenda seemed fair and unbiased. (A breakdown of the jury members and a note on recruitment methodology was attached to the original report as appendix two.)

2. The question

The question the jury was asked to consider was:
Where should women with gynaecological cancer who live in East Sussex, Brighton & Hove be offered treatment?

Jurors were asked to consider three options:

- To continue services in the current format.
- To centralise services in Brighton.
- To refer women for treatment at specialist cancer centres outside the county.

The jury met for an introductory evening on 20 February, and then for four days from 22 to 25 February 1997.

3. The evidence

3.1. Introductory evening

Jurors were welcomed by Alan Bedford, Chief Executive of East Sussex, Brighton & Hove Health Authority. They then spent some time getting to know each other and the facilitators. They heard about the background to the question and the role of the Health Authority from Graham Bickler, Director of Public Health.

3.2. Day 1 – setting the scene

Jurors were welcomed back by Kate Money, Director of Commissioning and Primary Care for Brighton and Hove. They then agreed a contract with each other and outlined their hopes, concerns and objectives. Their first witnesses were Anthea Barns and Hazel Thornton, who talked about their experience of cancer. Hazel stressed the importance of good information, the role of trials and that where you live can affect your cancer treatment and experience. Anthea talked about the importance of local access to treatment, quality of life and the support of family and friends.

After lunch, jurors heard from two witnesses who gave them some background to the question. Mike Richards, Clinical Director of Cancer Services at Guy's and St Thomas's NHS Trust, gave an overview of the Calman/Hine report and what it means for health authorities. He talked about the principles underpinning the report, which state that 'care should be provided as close to the patient's home as is compatible with high quality, safe and effective treatment'. He outlined the new structure for cancer services, which would involve primary care, cancer units in district general hospitals and cancer centres.

Jane Bridges, a consultant gynaecologist at the Chelsea and Westminster Hospital in London, gave information about the common gynaecological cancers (these are cancers of the vulva, the cervix, the uterus and the ovaries), how they present and the treatment offered. She also gave some information about the multidisciplinary team involved in providing care at the Chelsea and Westminster Hospital.

At the end of the day jurors worked in groups to look at what they had learned from four different perspectives: the patient; family and friends; care providers; and the health authority.

3.3. Day 2 – further scene setting

At the beginning of the day jurors heard from Zoe Nicholson, Commissioning and Primary Care Development Manager for the Health Authority. She talked about the needs relating to gynaecological cancer, the way services are currently delivered in East Sussex, Brighton & Hove and the issues and dilemmas facing the Health Authority. She also outlined how current services perform against the criteria outlined in the Calman/Hine report.

Jurors then heard from Henry Kitchener, Professor of Gynaecological Oncology at the Central Manchester NHS Trust. He presented the view of the joint working group of the Royal College of Obstetricians and Gynaecologists and the British Gynaecological Cancer Society on the Calman/Hine report. He argued that surgical specialisation leads to better outcomes for patients, and that gynaecological cancer centres should be based within cancer centres.

3.4. Option one – continue services in the current format

After lunch, jurors heard from Barry Auld, consultant gynaecologist at Hastings and Rother NHS Trust. He spoke on behalf of his own Trust and Eastbourne Hospitals NHS Trust, in favour of retaining the services in their current format. He argued that there is no evidence to show that specialisation is more effective in the treatment of gynaecological cancer (except in ovarian cancer), and that the service should remain local, with consultants referring on to specialist centres where they felt this was appropriate. He stressed the importance of local access, particularly for older patients. Hastings and Rother consultants currently work closely with the Royal Marsden Hospital and refer patients there. He stated that it would not be possible for local hospitals to become centres of excellence for gynaecological surgery because they do not deal with enough cases.

3.5. Option two – centralise services in Brighton

Jurors heard evidence from Andrew Fish, consultant gynaecologist from Brighton Health Care NHS Trust. He spoke in favour of centralising services at the Royal Sussex County Hospital through the development of a gynaecological cancer centre. He gave jurors a copy of a leaflet produced by the Cancer Relief Macmillan Fund, which advises women about the key question they should ask about their treatment [supplied in the original report as appendix three]. He advised jurors that Brighton could answer 'yes' to all of the questions. He informed the jury that Brighton might become a cancer centre for the common cancers, and that the oncology centre is being expanded. He also told jurors that Brighton is one of two centres that have been shortlisted to become a medical school. He outlined his work on gynaecological cancer and said that Brighton would need to treat women from East and West Sussex if it is to fulfil the criteria laid out in the Calman/Hine report. If it does not do this, it would not be a cancer centre and many women with gynaecological cancer would need to be referred outside the county.

3.6. Option three – refer women for treatment at specialist cancer centres outside the county

On day 3, jurors heard from Shanti Raju, consultant gynaecologist at Guy's and St Thomas's NHS Trust. She spoke about the audit she had conducted across seven health districts in the south of England to assess whether clinicians have followed agreed guidelines in the management of gynaecological cancers and the effect of inappropriate management on survival. She recommended treatment in specialist cancer centres, arguing that factors influencing the outcome for the patients include the involvement of a specialist surgeon, multidisciplinary teamwork and appropriateness of care. All of these are offered in specialist centres. Her audit showed that, although guidelines were developed by consensus, their implementation was poor and that there were high levels of inappropriate management of gynaecological cancer. She argued that transport was only one cause of stress for patients.

3.7. Further evidence from users

Jurors heard from three local women who have experienced gynaecological cancer. Donna had ovarian cancer and went to Pembury and the Kent and Sussex Hospitals. Fran had cervical cancer and attended Eastbourne and the Royal Sussex County hospitals. Cheryl had ovarian cancer and attended Lewes Victoria, the Royal Sussex County and the Royal Marsden Hospitals. Jurors then worked in small groups with these witnesses, who were assisted by a further three women who have experienced gynaecological cancer – Anthea, Brenda and Valerie. They explored each of the options outlined in the question and fed back their views on each.

Option one – to continue services in the current format
- Expertise is fragmented across the county.
- Further expenditure on the current set-up will not increase effectiveness.
- A centre of excellence is the preferred option – wherever it is.

Option two – to centralise services in Brighton
- Users' experience of the environment is poor.
- What improvements can be made to equipment and premises if we go for this option?
- Would it be viable to consider building a new centre in a different location – perhaps in Eastbourne?

Option three – to refer women for treatment at specialist cancer centres outside the county

- This is not a viable option. Concentrating on London will never improve the standards of care and treatment in East Sussex.
- We should spread the load and not send all patients to London.
- Patient choice is an important factor. London should be used to offer patients a second opinion, or as an alternative.
- If you refer all women to London, family and friends are a long way away.

Martina Pickin, Commissioning and Primary Care Assistant for Brighton, Hove & East Sussex Health Authority then reported back on some work undertaken jointly by the National Cancer Alliance and the Health Authority to listen to the experience and views of fifteen women in the area who have had gynaecological cancer. She described women's issues and concerns about the GP; referral to hospital; diagnosis; treatment and aftercare. Martina explained that women's experiences were very varied, ranging from excellent to appalling. It was often whom the women saw that played a key part in their experience. The role of the GP was seen to be particularly important for women with suspected ovarian cancer. Use of private health care also seemed to have the advantage of getting women into the system early, as did being a member of NHS staff. Finally she outlined what women said they wanted from a gynaecological cancer service. Jurors then had a further discussion with Martina and the user witnesses.

4. Considering the evidence

4.1. Additional witnesses

On day 4, jurors heard from three additional witnesses they had decided to call to help them to reach a decision. The first of these was Graham Bickler, Director of Public Health, whom the jury recalled to clarify some questions about the Health Authority's role as a purchaser of services. These included:

- Whether the Health Authority could use contracts to ensure adherence to best practice guidelines.
- Funding for improvements to the environment in which care is offered.
- The availability of equipment to treat more women with gynaecological cancer at the Royal Sussex County Hospital.
- The possibility of siting a gynaecological cancer centre outside the centre of Brighton.

- Access to services at the east of the county.

The second additional witness was Ashley Adsett, the cancer counsellor at the oncology centre at the Royal Sussex County Hospital. The jury asked her to address questions about:

- Plans for training additional nurse counsellors.
- The increasing demands on the oncology centre if Brighton were to become a gynaecological cancer centre.
- How she publicises her services.
- Whether she initiates contact with patients or waits for them to contact her.
- The importance of counselling for gynaecological cancer patients.
- At what point counselling is offered, and to whom.
- The possibility of training ward nurses as counsellors.
- An explanation about the work of the oncology centre.
- Whether it is possible for services to go to the patient, rather than the patient going to the services.
- The equipment and environment at the oncology centre and the plans to improve these.
- Information offered to family and friends.

The third additional witness was Peter Williams, a fundholding GP from Eastbourne. Jurors asked him to address questions about:

- The choices offered by the GP to a woman suspected of having gynaecological cancer.
- How up to date GPs are with the latest developments in the development of gynaecological cancer.
- Access to a database of information about symptoms.
- Views on centralisation of cancer services.
- The potential for Eastbourne to develop as a gynaecological cancer centre.
- The choice between local access and a centre of excellence.
- The use of counsellors in primary care.

5. Jurors' recommendations

During the remainder of day 4, jurors worked together to agree their vision for the future, their recommendations and the principles underlying them, and the concerns they wished to express to the Health Authority.

5.1. Principles underlying the recommendations

- The importance of a collective point of view shared by users and the majority of clinicians.
- The need to provide the best possible treatment for patients both medically and emotionally.
- Maintaining a balance between what is achievable and what is ideal, without losing sight of the ideal.
- Assisting current administrators to take a fresh look at all aspects of the care offered currently, with an eye to improvement.
- Progress should be achieved on a principle of negotiation.

5.2. The jurors' vision

In the long term, jurors would like to see a centre of excellence for cancer prevention, diagnosis, care, treatment and cure, located with space for further growth and alongside a supportive teaching hospital. They asked the Health Authority to explore potential sites for this, including disused psychiatric hospitals and land around the universitites.

5.3. Recommendations to the Health Authority about the current provision

- To address the discrepancy in standards in waiting times, facilities (particularly access to adequate car parking), clinical protocols and practice. Jurors stressed the importance of access to counsellors from the moment that the GP tells a woman that she may have gynaecological cancer.
- To ensure that treatment rooms are made more comfortable and private.
- To influence the review and unification of data collection, leading to the analysis of problem areas and uniformity of procedures.
- To encourage more specialist training about gynaecological cancer for the multidisciplinary team.
- To standardise procedures and practices in line with developing best practice.

5.4. The process of centralisation

Jurors were unanimous in their recommendation that the Health Authority centralise services within the county. They recommended the Health Authority to:

- Invest in the multidisciplinary team, premises and equipment at the Royal Sussex County Hospital as an interim cancer centre.
- Ensure that a system is put in place in associate units to take care of cases where routine surgery discloses cancer.
- Ensure adherence to best practice protocols, if necessary by encouraging a change of culture.
- Continue to support innovation, research and participation in trials.
- Ensure that data is up to date and centralised.

5.5. Jurors' concerns

Jurors also asked the Health Authority to note their concern that:

- Current provision is fragmented.
- Some doctors are ignoring best practice guidelines, and the current culture allows them to do this.
- There is a lack of good data.
- The current site at the Royal Sussex County Hospital is not an appropriate cancer centre because of the built-up nature of the environment and the difficulites involved in reaching and parking at the hospital.

6. Jurors' views of the process and the issue

The Health Services Management Centre issued a questionnaire to assess jurors' views at the beginning and end of the jury. [A summary of the results was attached to the original report as appendix four; facilitators' comments as appendix five.]

7. Next steps

This report was presented to a public meeting of the East Sussex, Brighton & Hove Health Authority on 29 April 1997, when jurors commented on their recommendations and on the jury as a whole. The Health Authority made an initial response to the jurors and to this report at that meeting.

8. Further information

A transcript of the jury, copies of the agenda and all handouts given to jurors are available from the project manager, Zoe Nicholson, at East Sussex, Brighton & Hove Health Authority, 36–38 Friars Walk, Lewes BN7 2PB.

Appendix 3

Buckinghamshire Health Authority Citizens' Jury: Report

1. Background

1.1. What is a citizens' jury?

A citizens' jury is a new way to involve the public in decisions that affect them in their local communities. Small groups of people are selected at random to reflect the local population. They meet over a period of four days to deliberate upon a question. They are informed about the issue, hear evidence from witnesses and cross-examine them, then discuss the matter amongst themselves and reach a decision or set of recommendations. A jury's decision is not binding, but it must be responded to publicly and taken into account in the decision making process of the organisation that sponsors it.

1.2. The King's Fund citizens' juries programme

In 1996 the King's Fund, an independent health charity based in London, launched a major grants initiative to examine the role of citizens' juries as a tool to involve local people in decision making about health care. Buckinghamshire Health Authority was one of three health authorities to be awarded a grant to organise a citizens' jury. In addition, the Health Services Management Centre at the University of Birmingham was commissioned to evaluate this work.

1.3. Background to the question

Buckinghamshire Health Authority identified the management of back pain as a key area in its 1996/97 corporate contract. Estimates extrapolated from the national Clinical Standards Advisory Group report on back pain showed that the NHS costs of back pain in Buckinghamshire were at least £5.5. million. The Authority wishes to ensure that the care purchased for back pain sufferers will give them maximum benefit and offer the best value for money for the local population. The citizens' jury appeared to offer an appropriate model for asking the public to help to weigh up a complex array of evidence, including clinical effectiveness, equity, accessibility, patients' views and experience, and public values.

1.4. Planning the jury

The Health Authority set up a steering group of local people to help to plan the jury. This consisted of representatives from the community health council, the local Back Pain Association, a GP, a local trust, Health Authority staff and a fieldworker from the King's Fund. [A list of steering group members was attached to the original report as appendix one.] Sixteen jurors were recruited to represent the population of Buckinghamshire. Fifteen of these took part in the jury. SMSR, a market research company, undertook the recruitment using a combination of methods. [A breakdown of the jury members and a note on recruitment methodology is attached to the original report as appendix two.] Two focus groups were held to check that the question to be put to the jury was understandable, and that the agenda seemed fair and unbiased. The King's Fund supplied two facilitators for the jury, Stella Davies and Bob Sang.

1.5. The electronic citizens' jury

The steering group worked with Colin Finney, research fellow at the Science Museum, to set up an electronic citizens' jury that would run alongside the existing jury. Evidence heard by the jurors was put onto the Internet and comment was invited from Buckinghamshire residents. This project received an additional grant from the King's Fund. (A report of this jury is available – please see section 8 of this report.)

2. The question

The question the jury was asked to consider was:
Should Buckinghamshire Health Authority fund treatment from osteopaths and chiropractors for people with back pain?

If 'yes', given that
(a)   these services are not currently purchased by the Health Authority
and
(b)   no extra resources are available for back pain services
    should some of the money we currently spend on physiotherapy be spent on osteopathy and chiropractic?

The jury met for an introductory evening on 7 March, and then for four days on 8, 9, 12 and 13 March 1997.

3. The evidence

3.1. Introductory evening

Jurors were welcomed by Julie Wells, Director of Communication at Buckinghamshire Health Authority. They then spent some time getting to know each other and the facilitators and sharing what they knew about back pain and its treatment. They heard about the background to the question and the role of the Health Authority from Jackie Haynes, the Chief Executive, and heard a discussion between Jackie and Judith Harvey, Chair of the Local Management Committee about GP fundholding.

3.2. Day 1 – setting the scene

On day 1, jurors agreed a contract with each other and outlined their hopes, concerns and objectives. These were:

- To produce a set of recommendations on the alternative treatments for back pain for local people in Buckinghamshire.
- To provide recommendations that can, in practice, be taken forward by the Health Authority.
- To be happy with the result, enjoy the process and gain new knowledge.

They then worked with Gill Needham, the Research and Development Specialist, and Alison Hill, Director of Public Health at the Health Authority, to think about how health care decisions are made, and the questions that can be used to help make these decisions. One of the key issues was effectiveness. This led to a discussion about randomised controlled trials, recognised as the best way of measuring effectiveness. Jurors identified some criteria to help them to assess forthcoming evidence.

After lunch, jurors heard evidence from Alison Hill. She talked about back pain in Buckinghamshire. She described what happens to people with back pain, the services available and what they cost. She explained why the Health Authority wanted the jury to address this question.

Gordon Gadsby, a reviewer from the Cochrane Collaboration Musculoskeletal Group, gave evidence about treatments for back pain; which of these have been shown to be clinically effective, what is not known about these treatments and where there is evidence against their effectiveness. He stated that 90 per cent of people with low back pain recover within six weeks, and that there is evidence to show that manipulation is most effective between six and twelve weeks after the onset of back pain.

3.3. Day 2 – Evidence about the different physical therapies

3.3.1 Osteopathy

The first witness of the day was Cathy Hamilton-Plant, an osteopath who is president-elect of the Osteopathic Association of Great Britain. She described what osteopathy is; what it can do for people with back pain; the training of an osteopath; the effectiveness of osteopathy; how it differs from physiotherapy and chiropractic; and what it costs. She stated there is no evidence comparing the effectiveness of osteopaths with chiropractors and physiotherapists. She offered information about osteopaths working in NHS clinics (e.g. in Barnsley) as well as those offering NHS sessions in their private practice. She stressed the importance of seeing a patient as soon as possible after the onset of back pain.

3.3.2. Chiropractic

The second witness of the day was Raymond Broome, a chiropractor with extensive involvement in the Anglo-European College of Chiropractic. He described what chiropractic is; its history and development; education and research; what happens when a patient sees a chiropractor; the effectiveness and cost-effectiveness of chiropractic; how safe it is; and the differences between chiropractic, osteopathy and physiotherapy. He cited research stating that patients seeing a chiropractor recover more quickly than those seeing a physiotherapist.

3.3.3. Physiotherapy

After lunch, jurors heard from Susie Durrell, a representative of the Chartered Society of Physiotherapists and a specialist in back pain. She spoke about the role of the physiotherapist in the treatment of back pain; the training of physiotherapists; their effectiveness; and their important role in the prevention of the recurrence of back pain through advice and exercise. She cited new evidence showing that exercises recommended by a physiotherapist can reduce recurrence of back pain.

3.4. Evidence from service users

Jurors heard from two witnesses who have experienced back pain – Sally-Anne Rodbourn and Janet Maybin. They described their experience of treatment from GPs, physiotherapists, an orthopaedic surgeon and a chiropractor. Sally-Anne felt that exercises offered through a physiotherapist had been most helpful to her. Janet felt that a chiropractor had been most helpful. Both witnesses stressed that there is no such thing as a typical back pain sufferer. They offered two 'snapshots'. They talked about the importance of early access to treatment and the need for back pain sufferers to take an active role in the management of their pain. Jurors then worked in two groups with these witnesses to discuss their evidence further.

3.5. Evidence from a local orthopaedic surgeon

The first witness on day 3 was Nigel Henderson, Consultant in Trauma and Orthopaedic Surgery at Stoke Mandeville Hospital, with a particular interest in spinal injures and spinal surgery. He talked about back pain, the options for treatment and the patients who are seen by an orthopaedic surgeon. He stressed the importance of educating patients to manage their back pain and their lifestyle.

3.6. Financial evidence

Jurors heard from Chris Daws, Director of Finance at Buckinghamshire Health Authority, and Nigel Woodcock, Director of Finance at Northampton General Hospital. Chris talked about how money is distributed in the NHS and how Buckinghamshire Health Authority spends its money. Nigel talked about how trusts are funded. They then offered a role play, in which the Health Authority was planning to reduce spending on physiotherapy for back pain. They talked about the financial implications of this decision.

3.7. Evidence from a local GP

After lunch, jurors heard from Craig White, a local GP with an interest in back pain. He described what a GP looks for when a patient presents with back pain, and how many patients come to the surgery with back pain. He talked about his views on the existing back pain service in Buckinghamshire and his vision for the future, which emphasised the appropriate use of guidelines and the addition of osteopaths and chiropractors to the current service working in a multidisciplinary team.

3.8. Evidence from the National Back Pain Association

The final witness of the day was Ann Holgarth, Help Desk Nurse with the National Back Pain Association and a back pain sufferer. She receives 20–25 calls per day from back pain sufferers. She stressed the human cost of back pain and the importance of good quality information at an early stage. She also talked about the importance of early referral to physical therapy where appropriate.

4. Considering the evidence

4.1. Additional witnesses

On day 4, jurors heard from three additional witnesses they had decided to call to help them to reach a decision. The first of these was Alison Hill, Director of Public Health, whom the jury recalled to clarify some questions about the Health Authority's role in relation to research and the distribution of physiotherapists who specialise in back pain across the county.

The second additional witness was Angela Whitehead, Senior Occupational Adviser for BP/Mobil based at Hemel Hempstead. The jury called her to discuss the effects of back pain in the workplace and exploring the possibility of employing chiropractors. Jurors asked her about timescales, cost and access to choice. They also discussed waiting lists.

Jurors read about a similar clinic at Marylebone, established by the Parkside Community Trust. An acute and chronic low back pain service was set up in 1996 and includes osteopaths, chiropractors and physiotherapists working together with other clinicians to offer a multidisciplinary service. This information was given to jurors via the Internet citizens' jury.

5. Jurors' recommendations

During the remainder of day, groups of jurors worked together to agree their recommendations, the principles underlying them and the concerns they wished to express to the Health Authority. They were assisted by Charles Sears, a Salisbury GP and member of the Clinical Standards Advisory Group on Back Pain and the Royal College of General Practitioners Guidelines Development Group. Charles acted as a sounding board for the jury to help them test their ideas and recommendations.

5.1. Principles underlying the recommendations

- Informed patient choice.
- Early assessment and access to treatment.
- The importance of the gatekeeping role.

- A service available to everyone who needs it.
- The need to take the onus away from the GP through the development of guidelines about the management of back pain.
- The need to better use existing resources and to identify alternative sources of funding.
- The need to reduce waiting time for diagnosis and treatment at each stage in the process.

5.2. The jurors' vision

In the long term, jurors would like to see an integrated system based on early referral to a centre of excellence, with joint education and practice development. This would be supported by the use of guidelines in primary care, professional development and evidence-based practice, and underpinned by collaboration and public education in awareness about back pain.

5.3. Jurors' recommendations

5.3.1. To improve patient choice

In the next year the Health Authority should:

- Set up meetings with GP representatives to discuss and agree guidelines for an early diagnosis and referral system, with referral within two weeks of seeing the GP.
- Use these meetings to investigate the potential for establishing local back pain clinics similar to those at Barnsley or Marylebone.

In the longer term, the Health Authority should:

- Negotiate with physiotherapists to ensure their agreement to work with osteopaths and chiropractors.
- Initiate discussions with osteopathy and chiropractic organisations about local co-operation.
- Ensure that therapists within back pain clinics offer patients verbal and written information (such as the 'Back book') about back pain and its management.

5.3.2. To better utilise public funds and resources

In the next year, the Health Authority should:

- Conduct a feasibility study into the possibility of establishing a pilot project on the use of chiropractors and osteopaths in back pain clinics.
- Investigate the cost implications of such a pilot project.
- Investigate the cost implications of educating and raising the awareness of GPs and physiotherapists about the pilot project.
- Implement a steering group to establish a pilot project.
- Establish links with other relevant bodies and interest groups to forward the pilot project.
- Look at funding for the pilot project through savings made by the adoption of guidelines (e.g. savings in use of outpatient clinics or X-rays).
- Investigate alternative sources of funding from industry, the NHS Research and Development budget and the Social Security budget savings to finance back pain clinics in the longer term.
- Explore the possibility of introducing chiropractors and osteopaths into existing physiotherapy departments by transferring funding from physiotherapy posts as staff leave or through increased funding.
- Begin pilot projects on cross-training between physiotherapists, osteopaths, chiropractors and GPs
- Enhance public and professional understanding of the number of back pain sufferers and the extent of the problem.

In the longer term, the Health Authority should:

- Conduct high-quality research and clinical audit into the use of chiropractors and osteopaths in NHS back pain clinics, including monitoring and reviewing these services.
- Ensure wide implementation of the pilot projects, if they are successful.
- Assess GP and patient satisfaction with the pilot projects.
- Undertake a public awareness campaign about the causes of back pain.

5.3.3. To develop collaboration with and between professionals and practitioners

The Health Authority should:

- Agree to the development of a centre of excellence for back pain
- Investigate existing centres of excellence for back pain

- Set up a multidisciplinary working group to plan and oversee the activities of such a centre
- Establish and carry out research on:
  - how other health authorities have established centres of excellence for back pain;
  - potential cost savings of such a centre;
  - who might be prepared to financially support the development or running of such a centre.
- Formulate local guidelines for back pain assessment and control.
- Ensure earlier treatment for back pain sufferers to make sure that those with acute pain do not become chronic pain sufferers.

5.4. Jurors' concerns

Jurors also asked the Health Authority to note their concerns that:

- Their opinion might not be taken seriously.
- There might not be a will to change among professionals.
- There are myths about medicine that may hinder development.
- Professional bodies might block multidisciplinary working.
- That the development of a centre of excellence and the provision of osteopathy and chiropractic in the NHS might cause demand for NHS services to outstrip supply.
- There might not be funds available to set up further, permanent, projects based on the pilot projects.

6. Jurors' views of the process and the issue

The Health Services Management Centre issued a questionnaire to assess jurors' views at the beginning and end of the jury. [A summary of the results was attached to the original report as appendix four, and facilitators' comments as appendix five.]

7. Next steps

This report was presented to a meeting of the Buckinghamshire Health Authority on 23 April, when jurors commented on their recommendations and on the jury as a whole. The Health Authority made an initial response to the jurors and to this report at that meeting.

8. Further information

A transcript of the jury, copies of the agenda and all handouts given to jurors are available from the project manager, Gill Needham, at Buckinghamshire Health Authority, Verney House, Gatehouse Road, Aylesbury, HP19 3ET. A report on the electronic citizens' jury can also be obtained from Gill.